Mountain Biking the Wasatch and Uintas

By Gregg Bromka

ISBN 0-9624374-0-9

Robert J. Welsh, Managing Editor
Design and Production by Robb Barr
Cover Design by Newman Passey Design, Inc.

All written material, maps,
and photos (unless otherwise noted) by the author

Cover photo: Bart, Dorothy, Nick, and Murray on Wasatch Crest Trail.

First Printing 1989
10 9 8 7 6 5 4 3

Printed in the United States of America.

All cyclists are invited to direct comments and corrections to the author:

Gregg Bromka
P.O. Box 526039
Salt Lake City, UT 84152

Requests for mail order may be directed to:

Wasatch Book Distribution
P.O. Box 1108
Salt Lake City, UT 84110
(801) 575-6735

Contents

Uinta Trails

Appendixes

Foreword

IT WAS A YEAR AGO, in early spring, that we met for the first time. I had just completed a slide presentation and was heading for my car when Gregg approached, introduced himself, and asked if by any chance I was working on a guide to nearby mountain bike trails.

"No, but it's a great idea," I replied, and rattled on about the need for a book of nearby one-day rides. I argued that in introducing new trails it would both expand our enjoyment *and* reduce the pressure on those few routes known to everyone, that if researched closely and written well it would keep riders off private property and out of wilderness areas (thereby reducing the kinds of conflicts that often result in trail closings), that many other regions with far less riding potential than the Wasatch Front have such guidebooks, that . . . .

Gregg stopped me with a smile. "You don't have to convince me. In fact, I've been planning one for some time."

I must admit that at first I thought he was like those many would-be writers who have good ideas for books, and great intentions, but bog down in the attempt. Proceeding gently, I asked if he was aware of the arduous work involved—months of at-the-desk and on-road research, time-consuming interviews with property owners and government land bureaucrats, detailed trail analysis and assessment. "And then, after all *that*, you still have to write the book!"

To my surprise Gregg's expression did not change. I expected this litany of difficulties to dismay him, to save him the wasted effort of beginning a project he would not complete. But his reply was the same disarming smile, and a simple sentence: "Yeah, I've considered all that."

And so he had. As I was to learn over the following year, in occasional phone calls and shared meals and on short rides (to see if I could find and follow trails on his directions), he had prepared well for the task. A strong

geology background allowed him to add excellent description and ex-
planation of the forces that had created the countryside. An indefatigable
nature and good riding ability placed all possible routes within his reach.
And, perhaps most important, a sense of humor and ability to write helped
him to create an informative *and* readable text.

My thanks to Gregg for his efforts. And my wishes for happy cycling to
all of you.

Dennis Coello

Acknowledgements

This book has not been simply a result of my own dreams and desires but a cumulative effort of many people and groups who offered valuable time and information. Without their input this book would not have been possible.

I wish to express many thanks to the personnel of the following land management and government agencies, who provided trail and land status information, and for eagerly approving this project:

> Wasatch-Cache National Forest
> > Salt Lake, Ogden, and Kamas Ranger Districts
> Uinta National Forest
> > Pleasant Grove and Heber Ranger Districts
> Utah State Division of Parks and Recreation
> Pioneer Trail and Wasatch Mountain State Parks
> Salt Lake County Department of Planning and Zoning
> Davis County Planning Department
> Salt Lake City Department of Planning and Zoning
> Draper City Planning Department
> Salt Lake City Watershed Management
> University of Utah Department of Campus Planning
> Utah State Arboretum

My sincere gratitude to the following groups and organizations:

> Salt Lake Regional Trails Council
> Bicycle Utah
> N.O.R.B.A. (National Off-Road Bicycle Association), now
> > part of the U.S.C.F. (United States Cycling Federation)

Also, thanks are extended to the following ski resorts:

> Alta Ski Lifts
> Brighton Ski Resort
> Snowbird Ski and Summer Resort
> Solitude Ski Resort

Throughout the trails section of this book many businesses are highlighted. Each is recognized as both a sponsor of this guidebook and a promoter of mountain biking in north-central Utah. A listing of sponsors is provided in the back of the book.

On a more personal note, I wish to thank those friends and acquaintances who provided trail information, patiently stopped for photos, and often followed me on rides of unknown difficulty and destination.

The equivalent of a thousand thanks are extended to Bob Welsh and Robb Barr of Ancestry, Inc.: to Bob Welsh for offering hours of advice into the world of publishing, and for accepting and then managing this book's production in a more than timely and professional manner; and to Robb Barr for his adept skills in page layout and design.

And last but by no means least, a special thank you to Dennis Coello—friend, author, and avid cyclist (an understatement)—for not only writing the foreword to this book but for providing me with the professional guidance and moral support to begin, pursue, and complete this project. Without his unyielding motivation, *Mountain Biking the Wasatch and Uintas* would have ended up in the circular file and not on the bookshelves.

Introduction

OVER THE YEARS the Wasatch Mountains have gained a reputation as one of the finest locations in the world for alpine and nordic skiing. During the warm summer months, many of those same great ski trails become popular routes for the recreational and devoted hiker and equestrian. Today, with the advent of the mountain bike, the Wasatch along with the Unita mountains have become havens for those outdoor adventurists choosing to explore the backcountry pedalling on two wheels. Combine this magnificent mountain playground with a major metropolitan area only minutes away, and you have a combination unique to northern Utah. Where else can you disappear deep into the rugged but serene mountainscape for a day's adventure, and return to enjoy bustling city excitement that evening?

Both the Wasatch and Uinta mountains flourish with opportunities for the bicycling enthusiast. A vast array of dirt roads and hiking trails offer bicyclists the opportunity to venture deep into the backcountry faster than afoot, and into more remote areas than by motor vehicle. The mountain bike has clearly become the medium of choice for an ever-growing number of outdoor recreationists. Everything from gentle, four-wheel drive roads offering a playful cruise to narrow, exacting single tracks demanding the most precise riding techniques from excruciating uphill assaults to paint-shaker downhills, is available. These off-road cycling opportunities direct the mountain biker along barren and undulating ridgelines; through textbook glaciated bowls forested with thick evergreens and quaking aspens; across broad, open meadows blanketed with pastel wildflowers and tall grasses; and past some of the most unique, impressive, and rugged geology in the United States. The local terrain clearly defines, in the truest sense, the term "mountain biking".

"Now that I've spent my life savings on this high-tech hybrid of the ancient 'clunker,' where can I ride it?" Granted, exploring new locales is part of the adventure and excitement of mountain biking, but how many times had I asked myself the same question while pondering an array of topographic maps in search of a new destination? How often had I religiously followed that weaving dashed line on the map, only to discover the trail rerouted or abandoned, diving precipitously off the hillside, climbing toward the heavens along a path even a mountain goat would think twice about, or simply petering out into thickets where bushwhacking meant sacrificing my body and clothes, where turning around meant an even more monumental task? More than once I returned from a ride threatening to stow away my ATB and become an avid road cyclist. Yet, despite the frustration, I'd load it up again and head out the very next day—often for more of the same.

The intended purposes of this guidebook are to alleviate the frustration associated with exploring new and enticing terrain, to provide trail information so the cyclist can set out onto new trails safely and with some knowledge of what lie ahead, and to promote off-road cycling as an environmentally acceptable mode of travel in a favorable light to other trail users. It describes many of the well-known (and a few not so well-known) off-road bicycling routes within an hour and a half drive of metropolitan Salt Lake City. Rides are arranged according to location (north to south), beginning with trails along the Wasatch Front (North Ogden through the Central Wasatch Tri-Canyon area to American Fork Canyon), followed by routes among the Lower Uinta Mountains (Kamas area through Strawberry Reservoir). Appendix 1 lists rides according to difficulty. The small-scale reference maps in the front and back of the book provide the general location of each trail; whereas, individual maps detail each trail description.

So pick a trail, a familiar one close to you or an intriguing route passing through unknown terrain, and experience the joy and exhilaration of mountain biking. Ride clean, ride smart, be courteous, and by all means *have fun!*

Mountain Biking

Trail Etiquette

PERHAPS THE MOST CRUCIAL ISSUE facing mountain bicyclists today is trail etiquette, a subject that cannot be overemphasized.

The advent of the mountain bike has been a boon to a once stagnant bicycle industry. In Salt Lake City, in particular, sales are tremendous, and the number of mountain bicyclists is skyrocketing. The result is a large increase in the number of trail users. Unfortunately, in the eyes of many non-bicycling trail users, off-road cycling is a destructive and offensive means of abusing our public lands, one that recklessly scars our pristine backcountry environment. Their case is warranted in a few situations: bikers riding dangerously fast and out of control; locking up brakes while kicking up a rooster tail of dust; shortcutting switchbacks; and blazing new trails across virgin meadows. Obviously, this kind of cycling cannot be tolerated.

Whether hikers, equestrians, or bicyclists cause more damage to the environment is an issue of great debate; one that attempts to discern who causes greater erosional damage and should therefore be excluded from enjoying the outdoors. The issue should focus on how all trail users can co-exist in the backcountry by working together to preserve what they have, and educating each group to the needs and desires of others so all groups might enjoy the outdoors to the same extent. For mountain bicyclists, the answer is simple: pay greater attention to trail etiquette—ride clean, ride smart, and be courteous. Since mountain bikers are "the new kid on the block," it is imperative that they improve their reputation and gain the respect of all other trail users. This can be accomplished by following a few simple guidelines.

Below is a compilation of the N.O.R.B.A. (National Off Road Bicycling Association) Code and mountain bike guidelines prepared by the Salt Lake Ranger District of the Wasatch-Cache National Forest:

1. Yield the right of way to other non-motorized recreationists. People judge all cyclists by your actions. Move off the trail to allow horses to pass and stop to allow hikers adequate room to share the trail.

2. Slow down and use caution when approaching another and make your presence known well in advance. Simply yelling "bicycle" is not acceptable.

3. Maintain control of your speed at all times and approach turns in anticipation of someone around the bend. Be able to stop *safely* within the distance you can see down the trail.

4. Stay on designated trails to avoid trampling native vegetation, and minimize potential erosion by not using wet or muddy trails or shortcutting switchbacks. Avoid wheel lockup. If a trail is steep enough to require locking wheels and skidding, dismount and walk your bike. Locking brakes contributes to needless trail damage. Do not ride cross-country. Water bars are placed across trails to direct water off the trail and prevent erosion. Ride directly over the top or dismount and walk your bike.

5. Do not disturb wildlife or livestock.

6. Do not litter. Pack out what you pack in and carry out more than your share whenever possible.

7. Respect public and private property, including trail use signs, no trespassing signs, and leave gates as you found them. If your route crosses private property, it is *your* responsibility to obtain permission from the landowner. Bicycles are excluded from designated Wilderness Areas.

8. Always be self sufficient. Your destination and travel speed will be determined by your ability, your equipment, the terrain, and the present and potential weather conditions.

9. Do not travel solo in remote areas. Leave word of your destination and when you plan to return.

10. Observe the practice of minimum impact bicycling. "Take only pictures and leave only waffle prints".

11. Always wear a helmet.

12. If you abuse it—you lose it! Since mountain bikers are newcomers to the forests, they must prove to be responsible trail users.

These guidelines are simple, basic common sense, but the message is clear: Ride smart, ride clean, be courteous, and by all means have fun. Make it your responsibility to propel mountain bikers to the forefront of the environmentally conscious and concerned.

Allowing others the right of way results in positive trail interactions.

Take Care of the Environment

A topic of equal importance as trail etiquette is general care for the environment. This means taking added measures and precautions to preserve your natural surroundings. Be aware of how your actions impact on the land off the trail as well as on it.

Many locations, especially the more distant Uintas, make for enjoyable multi-day outings. When camping on public lands, use developed campgrounds when ever possible; otherwise, choose a site that is several hundred feet from roads, trails, and water sources. This not only assures your own privacy, but lowers the noise and visual pollution others are trying to escape. Avoid fragile areas such as meadows and stream banks that cannot rejuvenate themselves easily.

Practice the technique of "Leave No Trace." Use camping stoves whenever possible; otherwise, use existing fire rings or follow proper methods to build and then cover new fire pits. Remember that the Wasatch and Uintas reach high levels of fire danger by mid-summer. Of course, carry out all trash and dispose of waste properly. Contrary to popular belief, orange peels and peanut shells take a long time to decompose and should never be left behind. Litter is a form of multiple pollution—physical, chemical, and visual.

Finally, although a peculiar and awkward subject to discuss, use discretion when defecating. Toilet facilities are placed at or near many popular trailheads—use them. But if necessity strikes while on the trail, move off the trail staying well away from water sources, dig a hole about eight inches deep in dark organic soil, then cover it completely. There is nothing worse than seeing rosettes of tissue paper budding from behind a rock or in the middle of a trail. Take a little extra time to keep your backcountry beautiful.

Land Ownership

FOR THE MOST PART, the trails and roads presented exist on National Forest Lands under the jurisdiction of the Wasatch-Cache National Forest (Salt Lake, Ogden, and Kamas Ranger Districts) and the Uinta National Forest (Heber and Pleasant Grove Ranger Districts). All trails mentioned are common routes that have existed and have been utilized by the public since people began venturing into the backcountry.

Yet, in the central Wasatch Mountains in particular, land ownership is still a patchwork of public and private property. Some trails cross small parcels of private property en route to or in the middle of public lands, a situation most common along trails adjacent to urban areas. In this case, it is the responsibility of the bicyclist to obtain permission from the landowner before crossing private property. Always obey the wishes of a property owner, respect all posted signs, and leave gates as you found them.

Although bicycles are generally accepted in the backcountry, a few special land policies need to be addressed.

United States Forest Service (U.S.F.S.)

Currently, the U.S.F.S. maintains an open policy toward mountain bikes. Bicycles are allowed on all designated hiking trails and roads unless otherwise posted. Be aware that these trails or roads are not constructed nor are they maintained specifically for bicycles. Thus, hazards and obstacles in or along a trail that may seem trivial to hikers, equestrians, or four-wheel drive vehicles may be significant to bicyclists. The responsibility again falls on the shoulders of the cyclist: ride within your own limits and abilities, have prior knowledge of the terrain, and plan your trip carefully. If in doubt about a trail's condition or difficulty inquire locally, ask a friend, or contact the U.S.F.S. Ranger District in that particular area.

The Salt Lake Ranger District has compiled a mountain bike trails inventory that discusses all off-road bicycling possibilities in the Wasatch-Cache National Forest along the central Wasatch Front. This inventory gives information on trail difficulty, conditions, access, and whether a particular trail is a recommended bicycling route. It is an excellent supplement to the information presented in this guidebook.

Wilderness Areas

At the present time, bicycles are prohibited from designated Wilderness Areas in accordance with the Wilderness Act of 1964. The issue is one of debate but will not be expounded upon here. Simply speaking, bicycles are mechanical means of transportation—even though the energy source is the human body—and thus are not allowed in Wilderness Areas. Don't compound the issue, stay out. Besides, along the Wasatch Front the four Wilderness Areas (Mount Olympus, Twin Peaks, Lone Peak, and Mount Timpanogos) offer terrain overall unsuitable to mountain bikes.

Front Range Watershed Areas

Bicycles are not restricted from any of the front range canyons that provide water to the city. However, be aware that domestic animals, i.e., pets, horses, and grazing animals, are not allowed in Big or Little Cottonwood canyons, Mountain Dell Canyon, nor City Creek Canyon, except through special permits. Since these canyons provide the majority of culinary water to the Salt Lake Valley, it is extremely important to keep them clean. Presently, pets and horses are allowed in Mill Creek Canyon as the water derived from this drainage is used mainly for agricultural purposes. Yet, both Mill Creek and Emigration canyons may join the others as protected watershed areas in the near future.

City Creek Canyon

City Creek Canyon, presently under the jurisdiction of both the U.S.F.S. and Salt Lake City Watershed Management, is an important source of the city's culinary water. It is managed both as a watershed and a wilderness area. The present policy for recreational canyon use is as follows.

During the summer season from Memorial Day weekend through the end of September:

- Foot traffic on the paved canyon road is allowed every day.
- Pets are allowed but must be on a leash. Above about 2.5 miles, pets and domestic animals are strictly forbidden.
- Motor vehicles are allowed on even days.
- Bicycles are allowed on odd days only, and they are excluded on all holidays whether an even or odd day. Currently, the City Creek Master Plan forbids all off-road bicycling within the canyon. Bicycle travel is restricted to the paved canyon road. Due to excessive erosion and trail user conflicts, the cross-country ski trail (once an excellent beginner/intermediate ride) has been closed to bicycles. In addition, the short dirt road extending from the top of Rotary Park is now off limits as it accesses the upper canyon (managed as a Wilderness Area), and the pipeline trails descending into the canyon from the adjacent ridgelines have been closed due to erosion and dangerous trail conditions. These represent the first trail closures along the Wasatch Front. Let's hope they are isolated incidents. Only smart, clean riding will prevent more trail closings in the future.

During the winter months:

- Vehicles are prohibited.
- Ski and bike travel on the paved canyon road is not encouraged due to heavy machinery and snow removal equipment maintaining access to the water treatment plant.

Please note that officials of the Salt Lake City Watershed Management have the authority to fine any violator, and that pamphlets covering City Creek Canyon use are available at the information board at the entrance gate to the canyon.

Utah State Division of Parks and Recreation

Wasatch Mountain State Park allows bicycles on its two-wheel drive and four-wheel drive dirt roads. Dirt roads within Pioneer Trail State Park, on the other hand, are part of Old Deseret, a reconstructed pioneer community representing the period from 1847 to 1869. For the protection of horsedrawn vehicles and pedestrains, bicycling on these roads is not encouraged.

Ski Resorts

The four ski resorts in Big and Little Cottonwood canyons (Brighton and Solitude, Alta and Snowbird, respectively) are ideal for mountain biking. Four-wheel drive access roads crisscross the ski resorts and provide cyclists the opportunity to rise high up onto the mountain peaks while passing through hillsides blanketed with wild flowers and cut by clear, icy streams. All resorts operate under permits issued by the U.S.F.S., and thus fall under the Forest Service's guidance. Within each resort, mining claims and summer homes exist. Any man made structure, whether related to the resort or not, should be respected as private property.

Contrary to popular belief, the ski resorts do not board up their windows and close down for the summer. Use caution when riding ski access roads as heavy machinery and resort equipment may be present and maintaining trails, lifts, and structures at any time. Always be aware of any activity occurring up-slope of the trail you are on, since crews may not know of your presence.

Terrain

MANY ARE CONTENT with tunneling their vision down the five foot wide dirt path, scanning for obstacles to negotiate, while a dynamic world of towering peaks, verdant trees, and delicate flowers pass by unnoticed like a blurred rainbow. Here the attraction of a ride is strictly a measure of the immediate challenges presented: how steep are the climbs, how fast can I cruise back down, and what obstacles contribute to the trail's difficulty and can they be negotiated without touching a foot down? Without question, these are some of the thrills of mountain biking, the factors that contribute to its overwhelming exhilaration. Yet, off-road cycling offers so much more. More than the sheer physical challenge, mountain biking provides a new medium for exploring the far reaches of the backcountry, to venture into new and enticing terrain that otherwise may go unnoticed. Enjoy the excitement and stimulation associated with off-road riding, but slow down, stop occasionally, an let the surrounding environment captivate you.

Utah is a geologist's paradise. Coined not only the Beehive State but also the Bedrock State (Stokes, 1986), great expanses of exposed rock formations can turn the every day hiker, biker, or equestrian into an inquisitive geologist seeking to reveal the events of the past recorded in the millions of years of lithified history.

On a grand scale, the state of Utah sits among four major physiographic provinces: the Colorado Plateau, the Middle Rocky Mountains, the Basin and Range Province, and the Colorado Plateau/Basin and Range Transition. The Wasatch Range and the Uinta Mountains mark the western border of the Middle Rocky Mountains, whereas the Wasatch Front denotes the eastern-most extent of the Basin and Range Province. Also, the Salt Lake and adjacent valleys lie on the smooth saline floor of the ancient and once expansive glacial Lake Bonneville.

Narrow glacial valleys and sharp ridgelines characterize the Wasatch Range.

Extending over 200 miles in length, the Wasatch Line, synonymous with the Wasatch Fault and Wasatch Front, is the backbone of Utah, one of the most important geologic features in North America. Not only does the Wasatch Front mark the western boundary of the Middle Rocky Mountains and the eastern border of the Basin and Range, its complex geologic setting is unique only to itself as no other occurrence of its kind exists in the world. Some of the longest normal faults have been mapped along its length.

The Wasatch Line itself consists of a series of parallel, en echelon, faults—a zone of crustal weakness where igneous activity was concentrated and where earthquakes and hot springs are still common. Its facade is impressive and seemingly impenetrable, as the Earth's crust has been uplifted over three miles, where peaks rise 7,000 feet above the present valley floor. Behind the Front, the Wasatch Range is a tilted fault block (in simplest terms), but upon closer inspection its complexity is revealed.

The area now occupied by the Wasatch Range was once a zone of sedimentary accumulation—a broad depression where sediments, washed in from adjacent highlands, were deposited in a shallow marine environment. Alternating layers of limestones, shales, and sandstones suggest the ancient sea level fluctuated, while periods of uplift and subsidence stripped off exposed layers then again blanketed the basin with fresh sediments. At least once throughout geologic history, the Wasatch Range coincided with the ancient Pacific Ocean shoreline.

**The Wasatch Mountains truely define the term
"mountain" biking.**

A first mountain building phase bulged and uplifted the mass, folding and faulting the sedimentary units. Simultaneously, huge segments of rock were transported not only vertically along high angle normal and reverse faults but laterally along low angle "thrust" faults. Mount Timpanogos, with its characteristic horizontal layering, is believed to have been transported as an entire unit to its present location from areas miles to the west near Rush and Cedar Valleys. Termed the Charleston-Nebo Thrust, this type of low angle, horizontal displacement is also common among the mountains east of Ogden.

Following this deformation, the Wasatch Fault (a zone of structural weakness trending southwest to northeast along a great curved arc) uplifted the rock mass, tilting it to the east and northeast. An excellent example of the powerful deforming forces acting in the Earth's crust is displayed in Little Cottonwood Canyon across from Snowbird Resort. Here, the banded gray and white limestones comprising the Hellgate Cliffs (Mississippian Age) have been down faulted to where they are in contact with and below the older (Precambrian) tan and brown quartzites and shales of the Big Cottonwood Formation comprising Mount Superior to the west.

After the range was raised to its present height, igneous activity emplaced bodies of once molten granite-like rocks into the sedimentary strata, forming the gray cliffs and peaks at the mouth of Little Cottonwood Canyon (Little Cottonwood stock) and between Alta and Brighton (Alta and Colton stocks). Finally, in most recent geologic time (Pleistocene or the "Ice Age") high alpine glaciers and swift flowing mountain streams dissected the range, producing its present-day rugged topography. Of course, all the preceding geologic activity took place over the span of a meager 800 million years!

The Uinta Mountains, on the other hand, have a simpler geologic history, but are no less unique nor significant than the Wasatch Range: simple in that they are an uplifted mass of layered sediments originally deposited in a broad marine basin; unique in that their east-west trend is discordant not only to the Wasatch Range (intersecting it at right angles), but to the overall trend of the entire Rocky Mountain Region.

Dating back over 2 billion years, the Uintas mark a long period where sediments were washed into the broad Uinta Trench, a shallow marine environment, and lay essentially undisturbed until about 60 to 70 million years ago when they were uplifted along with the greater Rocky Mountain region. Bowed by compressive forces, the broad Uinta arch was fiercely attacked by erosive elements that stripped off 30,000 to 40,000 feet of overlying strata, such that only the oldest and deepest of rocks, the Precambrian Uinta Mountain group, still remain—those comprising essentially all of the Uinta highlands (Hansen, 1983).

Rising to over 13,000 feet above sea level, the Uintas boast the states highest peaks. Unlike the Wasatch Mountains, a chaotic assemblage of jagged peaks and narrow valleys, the Uinta peaks are broader and rise above expansive lofty plateaus. Glacial processes that produced the mountains' present day topography were more widespread where tongues of ice extended almost thirty miles; whereas in the Wasatch, most alpine glaciers were confined to less than five miles. In the Uintas, huge rock amphitheaters open up to wide, flat valleys pocked with thousands of tiny lakes and ponds and rimmed by towering vertical cliffs; whereas in the Wasatch Range, small glacial cirques, like a cuspate bite out of an apple, open up to narrow, steep U-shaped valleys (the characteristic shape of Little Cottonwood Canyon).

Conveniently located next to a major metropolitan area, the Wasatch-Cache National Forest is one of the most frequently visited recreation areas in the United States. At times the local mountains seem to be over-run with people seeking a bit of seclusion from life in the valley. Trails become thoroughfares, peace and quite are elusive. Yet, topographically and geologically distinct, the Uintas host unyielding opportunities for the mountain bike enthusiast with the desire to explore its myriad crisscross-ing logging roads. And, only an hour's drive from Salt Lake City, the Uin-tas are a convenient alternative for both an afternoon or multi-day outing.

There are basically two ways to cross a stream.

Never Ending
Possibilities

HOME OF THE ANNUAL Canyonland's Fat Tire Festival, the Moab area of Southern Utah hosts perhaps the most unique and unusual cycling environment in the world—slickrock, the petrified geologic remains of vast oceans of once drifting sand dunes, shoreline beaches, and broad river bottoms. Exemplifying this distinct riding medium is, of course, the Slickrock Trail—a ten-mile loop rolling along barren sandstone hills and bowls that requires exacting handling skills as you perform bicycle gymnastics with magnificent views of deep canyons, snow capped mountain peaks, and the lush Moab Valley. What makes slickrock so appealing is the traction, 100 percent pure traction, like riding over hills of rough sandpaper. Tilt your bike on edge, ride it off hills that are difficult to walk down, grunt up seemingly vertical walls without threat of slipping or spinning, and you've experienced the thrill of slickrock.

The autumn festival in Moab rivals that of other mountain bike fests throughout Colorado and California. It is a week long, non-competitive, social gathering of mountain bike enthusiasts of all ages and abilities where the emphasis is placed on having fun amidst a care-free atmosphere. An array of group rides, social gatherings, and evening activities highlight the event. Where else can you be part of a contingent of over 500 bicycle fanatics parading down Main Street, en route to a mass pancake breakfast before frolicking on the Slickrock Trail to participate in perhaps the world's largest game of poker?

This is not to say that the Canyonland's region is the only other enticing mountain biking location in the state. Several other regions around the state now host mountain bike festivals including the Castle Country and Fish Lake in the Fall Fat Tire Festivals of the Price, Utah, and Fish Lake National Forest regions, respectively. The recently published *Bicycle Utah Vacation Planner* highlights many on- and off-road cycling opportunities within each of Utah's nine travel regions and is available free of charge at most bike shops and travel information centers. In the near future, each travel region hopes to produce a small booklet detailing individual rides.

On a more local level, many bike shops host competitive races and social evening or weekend rides throughout the summer. But don't be intimidated if an event is labeled a "race." Categories for entrants range from first time/beginner riders to pro-am levels where the general atmosphere emphasizes fun and social camaraderie.

Overall, Utah hosts a wide array of diverse bicycling opportunities where each route varies and is more alluring than the last. Around the state you can find rugged mountaintop cycling along the Wasatch Range near Logan and the Idaho border, never-ending dirt roads winding through deep canyons and onto broad plateaus, or centuries old Anasazi Indian ruins near the southern reaches of the state, making Utah the potential bicycle vacation capital of the United States.

Parading down Main Street, Moab, during the Canyonland's Fat Tire Festival.

One of many outstanding vistas in Canyonlands.

The Self-Sufficient Cyclist

MOUNTAIN BIKING, more so than most recreational activities, requires you to know your limits—both physical limitations and riding skills. How far and how hard you can ride often determine where and when you can ride. Many routes take you miles from human contact and help, if needed. Thus, the individual rider, whether venturing out alone or with a group, must be able to handle any situation, repair, or emergency that may arise. In other words, be prepared for the unexpected.

Physical Conditioning

For those embarking for the first time, be forewarned: mountain biking can be a very strenuous activity, more so than road cycling, jogging, or hiking. Riding dirt trails and roads requires not only physical strength and stamina but high levels of balance, coordination, and concentration. Surely, mountain biking rates as one of the best forms of exercise. Anyone who claims bicycling is just not enough of a workout has not been on a mountain bike. After a long, rocky ascent lungs sear, legs burn, and sweat pours from your brow—it's a great feeling, especially knowing that only yesterday you couldn't quite make the climb, but today you've conquered it.

Whether a first time rider, or the first ride of the season, start easy and work your way up to the harder, more demanding rides. By progressively building your strength and endurance you'll find yourself grinding up trails that you would not have attempted previously. Yet, tackling a *gonzo* ride before you are ready may result in walking and pushing until the initial joy of adventure wears off and total frustration sets in—much like skiing deep powder but falling on every turn. So, the only way to enjoy mountain biking fully is to be physically conditioned, and the best way to condition your body is to get out and ride as often as possible.

Water and Food

Water and nourishment are essential. Typically, the summer months in northern Utah are hot and dry. Combine this with strenuous physical activity and you must pay close attention to your body's needs.

Even on cool days at high altitude dehydration can be a serious problem. Avoid it at all costs. Many rides do not cross a water source, so plan to carry all that you will need. If you are considering drinking stream or other surface water, be very careful. Although that crystal clear mountain stream looks clean, domestic and wild animals may have contaminated the waters with bacteria—it only takes one bout with bad water to prove the point. If in doubt, purify. Always carry more than you think you will need.

Food, on the other hand, is a personal matter. High energy bars, fruit (fresh or dried), or any variety of gorp or trail mix should suffice. Learn from your experiences but don't neglect your body's call for nourishment. "Hitting the wall," running out of gas, or just plain exhaustion is an uncomfortable feeling and possibly a dangerous situation. Rarely in the Wasatch will you be in any grave danger, but in the Uinta's, trails may take you twenty or more miles from civilization. Be safe, over estimate, the extra pound or so may be worth it. Better to return with a half full water bottle and a left over candy bar than face still miles of strenuous riding with a dry, parched throat and a dizzy head. Besides, with a little excess, you may be able to help out someone less fortunate who did not plan as carefully as you.

Pre-ride Planning

As important as being prepared physically and making sure all your equipment is together is planning your trip. Sure, half the joy of mountain biking is exploring new and unknown territories, but getting lost soon turns a fun ride into a potential nightmare. *Plan your trip.* Acquire the appropriate maps; familiarize yourself with the terrain, distances, and riding times expected; obtain a current local weather report; and leave notice with someone of your intended destination and time of return.

The details provided for each trail in this guidebook should answer

**Walking your bike is all part of the game, as some trails
are just too difficult in spots.**

most of the questions for a particular ride. If doubt still persists, inquire locally, go to a local bike shop, contact the U.S.F.S. District Ranger Office near you or near the trail locality, or ask a friend who has been on the ride previously. A variety of maps are available at the district ranger offices, the United States Geological Survey Map and Information Office in downtown Salt Lake City in the Federal Building, and at a number of outdoor and recreational stores throughout the valley.

Bicycle Maintenance

O.K., you've planned your trip, the weather looks good, and you've got lots of water and food. You're ready to go—or are you? Is your bike ready and in good working order? When did you last check it over, clean, and lubricate it? Are you your own bike mechanic? Remember, you and your bike act as one on the trail, so both must be in proper condition.

Bicycle maintenance is a subject that has been more than adequately covered in a variety of books and videos. Occasionally, classes are taught which provide valuable hands-on experience. Buy a book, take a class, and learn to be your own bicycle mechanic. If you refuse to learn even the minimal repair techniques then at least ride with someone who has learned them.

Check and clean your equipment before and after every ride. Repair or replace worn or broken parts immediately. Fixing a flat tire is one thing, but trying to rig a broken cable or tighten a loose headset is nothing to look forward to when you're miles from nowhere. Don't wait for a mishap on the trail to realize how little you know about your bike.

Tools and Repair Equipment

Don't ride empty handed, either. To be self-sufficient you must carry along at least a minimal amount of repair equipment, but you do not have to pack an entire tool box.

What you'll pack along may vary with the ride or the group you ride with. Learn from your experiences and mistakes and note what others bring. A short, easy ride has fewer risks than a full day tour through rough terrain, and usually it is not necessary to double up on equipment within the group you're traveling with.

Here are a few tools and accessories to consider:

- **Tire repair tools:** Tire levers and patch kit. Also, consider bringing a spare tube as multiple holes often go unnoticed. Remember to repair the flat tube at home instead of carrying it around with you for days.

- **Wrenches:** Essential if your hubs are not quick release.
- **Pump:** Make sure it fits both the valve stem (Shreader versus Presta) and the bike's frame securely. Cartridge inflators are quick, but they are only good for one use.
- **Adjustment tools:** Flathead and Phillips's screwdrivers, a variety of hex/Allen wrenches, adjustable or small vise-grip type pliers, and open end or box socket wrenches. Check your bike in detail for the proper size tools to fit all nuts, bolts, and screws.
- **Chain rivet tool:** To remove a broken or bent link, or shorten the chain to bypass a broken rear derailleur.
- **Spoke wrench:** To remove a broken spoke or to straighten a tweaked rim.
- **Spare cables:** A rear brake cable can always be cut to fit a front cable, or a long rear derailleur cable can be rigged to fit all other cables in most cases.
- **Swiss army knife or multipurpose tool:** Some of these can take the place of and are more compact and convenient than an assortment of loose tools.
- **Chain Lube:** A dry, dirty chain is not only a squeaky nuisance capable of producing a scowl from every passerby, but can be the source of hours of frustration as gears constantly skip and shift with a mind of their own. But, if you don't take the time to clean your chain and drive system at home, why bother on the trail, right?

A word of advice: If splitting the load of equipment among a group, stay fairly close together on the trail (at least within shouting or sight distance). Be aware of each other's abilities, and stop frequently to re-group. It does little good for the lead rider to be carrying the tire levers and patch kit if you're dragging miles behind when you have a flat.

Accessories

- **Helmet/brain bucket:** Like the American Express Card, don't leave home without it. And like a form of insurance, you hope never to have to use it, but when you need it you're sure glad you have it. Contrary to popular belief, it fits your head better than your handle bars or rear rack. Consider this a necessity, not an accessory.

The art of being self-sufficient.
(Photo by Dennis Coello.)

- **Water bottles and cages:** Have the ability to carry at least two over-sized bottles.

- **Rear rack/panniers:** For longer rides, panniers or bicycle bags are a luxury, whereas loose fitting backpacks or daypacks can be cumbersome and dangerous as their shifting weight can toss you right off your bike. Choose sturdy aluminum racks and high quality bags that fasten securely to the bike's frame. High quality panniers have compartments and compression straps to prevent enclosed items from shifting under sudden movements. A small under-the-saddle bag will accommodate all tools and fix-it equipment.

- **Fanny pack:** For those who do not like the sometimes awkward weight distribution and size of bicycle bags on narrow trails, a fanny pack secures items tightly to your body and prevents swaying of the additional weight.

- **Cyclometer or bicycle computer:** A multifunction bicycle computer is convenient to judge mileage, time, speed, etc., and is surprisingly durable. But, be sure to take up the slack in the power cord by wrapping it around the front fork, handle bars, or brake cable to prevent snagging on passing branches.

- **Lock:** Protect your investment. Even on backcountry trails, thieves lurk. If your trip is a combination bike and hike, lock it and carry along all valuables.

- **Camera:** To many this is a necessity not an accessory. Brilliant sunsets, spring wildflowers, autumn colors, changing cloud formations, and of course some of the most fantastic geology around are all worth photographing. Be sure to carry your camera on your body, i.e., secured in a fanny pack or by a chest harness (not dangling from your neck), as the pounding and vibration of hard riding will destroy it if stowed in a bike bag or strapped to a rear rack.

Clothing

Whether on the road or trail, the variety of cycling fashion is staggering, from T-shirts and cut-offs to color coordinated, one piece, stretch lycra suits. Clothing is obviously a personal matter, but consider function as well as style.

- **Padded bicycling shorts and gloves:** These not only cushion a bumpy ride but prevent chaffing and blistering.

- **Shirts:** For the most part, a cotton T-shirt will suffice during the summer months. When weather turns colder, a long sleeve shirt of a breathable synthetic material will keep you warm and dry.
- **Shoes:** Rugged but lightweight hiking shoes or mountain biking shoes have semi-rigid soles that provide support both in the pedals and on the trail.
- **Shells and extra layers:** A nylon or other breathable synthetic waterproof shell and stretch tights will protect you from unexpected climatic changes, are light weight and compact, and can be stuffed easily into a small bike bag or fanny pack.
- **Sunglasses/goggles:** Not only are sunglasses designed to be fashionable (an important feature for some people), they protect your sensitive eyes from harmful sun rays, passing branches, and flying mud. Make sure glasses are securely fastened with some type of eyeglass retention device or leash.
- **Sunscreen:** For those who insist on riding as scantly clad as possible to avoid embarrassing tan lines, sunscreen is a must. At high altitude, the atmosphere is thinner and offers less protection against the sun's burning rays. After only an hour or two the sun can fry you as red as a lobster, enough to ruin your whole day or vacation.

First Aid

Like wearing a helmet, you never hope to need first aid, but when you do you're sure glad you brought it. Cuts, scrapes, bumps, and bruises are not only a possibility, they should be expected. Flying rocks and protruding branches constantly batter away at exposed flesh. More serious injuries include sprained ankles, twisted knees, and broken fingers resulting from sudden dismounts upon crossing rugged terrain. A minimal amount of first aid will care for most situations. Most outdoor/recreational stores sell a variety of prepackaged, compact first aid kits, or you can create your own with an assortment of bandage strips, gauze pads, adhesive tape, mole skin, antibacterial towelettes or ointments, and pain relievers. Water purification tablets are essentially weightless and may save you days or weeks of "discomfort" from a bout with bad water.

NOW, your bike is ready, you've prepared yourself mentally and physically, your route is carefully planned, and you are bringing enough equipment to survive a nuclear holocaust, so *LET'S RIDE!*

Trail Description Format

FOR CONSISTENCY each trail is described according to a set format. Pertinent data is presented first, followed by a detailed trail description and a map. Occasionally, one map may be appropriate for more than one trail. Some trails have a representative photo accompanying each description. Format subheadings are described here in brief.

Trail Name

Trail names are consistent with those already established, otherwise they are based on prominent features labeled on U.S.G.S. 7.5' topographic quadrangles. Trail numbers, i.e., W-1, correspond to both individual trail maps and the general location maps on the inside front and back covers.

Location

A general idea of where the trail is located geographically, usually with respect to the closest town, city, or physiographic feature.

Access

A recommended route is suggested to the trailhead/parking area based upon established paved or dirt roadways. All routes are public use/access; all trails are within an hour and a half drive from Salt Lake City. Abbreviations include:

I-#:	U.S. Interstate highway
U.S. #:	U.S. highway
S.R. #:	State or local maintained paved road
F.R. #:	Forest Road (usually two- or four-wheel drive dirt, maintained or unmaintained)

Parking

A convenient parking location for support vehicles, again on public lands, is presented. Where a parking area is not suggested, it is due to private property limitations.

Trailhead

Usually at or near the parking area, the trailhead is the recommended starting point for a given ride. Mileages and times begin at this location.

Type

Three types of trails are common: loop (ridden in one direction with little or no back tracking); out and back (ride to the end of the trail, turn around, and double back); or combination (combined out and back with an integrated loop).

Also included in this category is the type or quality of path the trail follows:

2WD: maintained dirt/gravel road, passable by two-wheel drive vehicles (under most conditions);

4WD: unmaintained dirt/gravel road or trail, passable by vehicles with four-wheel drive (under most conditions),

Single track: maintained or unmaintained hiking trail or ATV trail where the tread is usually a narrow single path.

Land Status

The ownership of the land over which the trail proceeds is identified, usually U.S.F.S., but may include state, city, or private property.

Maps

Appropriate U.S.G.S. 7.5' topographic quadrangles and other helpful maps are noted. Topographic maps are available at the United States Geological Survey Map Office in the Federal Building, downtown Salt Lake City, or at a variety of outdoor, camping, and recreational equipment retail stores throughout the valley.

Length/Time

Mileages noted in bold (**m 0.0**) in the trail description correlate to those labeled on corresponding trail maps. Even though mileages may vary between brand name cyclometers, the cross reference between description and trail map mileages is helpful to locate important turns, trail conditions, or points of interest.

Time, in hours and minutes, is the amount of time it will take a rider of average to advanced ability to complete a ride *without* stops. Naturally, allow more or less time depending on your physical condition, riding skills, and need to stop and rest. What may take an aggressive, experienced rider two hours to complete, may take someone who emphasizes sightseeing all day. As you ride through the spectacular back country, do slow down and allow extra time to absorb the beautiful surroundings and ponder the wonders of nature.

Elevation Changes

In feet, elevations note the high and low points on a trail. The change is simply the difference between these two. This may be somewhat deceiving (i.e., on a ridgeline trail where the undulating path may have significant total elevation gains and losses, the change between the high and low points may be small). Trailhead elevations are presented to give the rider an idea where the trail starts with respect to the highest and lowest points on the ride.

Overall Difficulty

The amount of energy expended to complete a ride based primarily on length, technical difficulty, and elevation gains (overall and incremental).

Obviously, this is a very subjective rating. What is difficult for one rider may be easy for the next. Also, degree of difficulty is relative, i.e., trails are compared to other trails within this book. These may vary considerably from rides in other parts of the state or country. Riding a trail in the opposite direction of that presented may greatly change the difficulty. Categories include easy, easy/moderate, moderate, moderate/difficult, and difficult (and *gonzo* in a few cases).

Technical Difficulty

How often a rider is expected to dismount or set a foot down to negotiate a particular obstacle or hazard including, but not limited to, rocky terrain, unusually steep climbs or descents, ruts, logs, exposed roots, water bars, water crossings, severely eroded trails, etc. Again, this is a subjective, relative rating. Categories include minor, minor/moderate, moderate, moderate/technical, and technical.

Following overall difficulty and technical difficulty is a summary of the trail's conditions and attractions.

Description

As detailed as possible, the reader/rider will be lead along the trail like on a personal guided tour, while important changes in terrain (hills, descents, and obstacles), turnoffs, highlights, and attractions are noted. Most of these will be noted by mileages in bold (**m 0.0**) and cross referenced to the adjoining trail map. Since it is mainly the geology that makes the Wasatch and Uinta Mountains so distinct and attractive, prominent and sometimes overlooked geologic features in both the immediate vicinity and distant view will be emphasized. Slow down and absorb the surroundings instead of simply speeding along, tunneling your vision on a five foot wide path, while the magnificent countryside flashes by in a blur. In most cases, a representative photo accompanies each trail.

Options

Following the trail description are optional rides related to the main trail just described. Usually, these options are mentioned in brief or as suggestions for further personal explorations. Technical data for optional rides are included in parentheses: (type, length/time, elevation changes, overall difficulty, and technical difficulty). Mileages noted in bold in "Options" correspond to mileages in parentheses on trail maps.

Notes

Any supplementary information pertinent to the trail description is presented, i.e., unusual land status, important trail use policies, or trails joining or branching from the main route.

Trail map

Following each trail description is a map outlining the trail with mileage markers, parking (P) and trailhead (T) locations, and prominent physiographic features. Although U.S.G.S. 7.5' topographic maps are preferred, their large scale is difficult to reduce to book form, and smaller scale maps lack detail. These hand drawn maps are based on published topographic maps of varying scale and should be used as a general reference only. Carry along the standard 7.5' quads. (1:24,000) when venturing into unknown terrain. Also helpful in distinguishing land status, access, and U.S.F.S. trail and road numbers, are the U.S.F.S. Travel Plan Maps (scale: one inch equals about two miles) available at area Ranger District Offices. Consider also U.S.G.S. and B.L.M. metric topographic maps of a scale 1:100,000 (one inch equals approximately 1.6 miles).

Another word on maps. Quite often, trails labeled on a topographic map do not correspond to those on the ground or described here. Thus, understanding orienteering is to your advantage and strongly recommended, especially when venturing into new territories. Being able to distinguish and read landforms and pinpoint your whereabouts should keep you from getting lost in the event the trail you are riding does not correspond with that on the map. The heavily traveled and populated Wasatch Mountains pose little threat of getting lost, whereas the Uintas trails often venture miles from human contact.

Map Symbols

(80)	U.S. Interstate
(40)	U.S. Highway
(35)	State or local route
(54)	U.S.F.S. Forest road
——————	Paved roadway (U.S., state, or local)
— — — —	Dirt road (two- or four-wheel drive)
- - - - - - -	Single track (hiking trail)
··············	Bushwack/portage
(P T)	Parking/trailhead
W-5 W-5.1	Trail number (optional trail number)
1.5 (1.5)	Trail mileage marker (mileage for optional trail) Corresponds to mileages in bold in trail description
～～～ ···～～	Drainage-perrenial, intermittent
⌒⌒ ⬭	Spring, pond, or lake
·············△ 10172	Notable peak or hill with ridgeline (elevation in feet above sea level)
↜ᴧᴧᴧᴧᴧ	Cliff, steep escarpment
⬭	Snow field
•— — —•	Ski lift or tram
⊢———⊣	Gate or fenceline
— ·· — ·· — ·	Wilderness boundary
⬥	District Ranger Station
∎	Forest Service Station
⋏	U.S.F.S. campground
⬩	Radio facility
⚒	Quarry or mine
↺	Corral

Warning/Disclaimer

ALTHOUGH THIS BOOK mentions several trails "suitable" to bicycle travel, the author does not suggest that anyone in particular ride any route in particular. It is impossible to guess or judge someone's riding skills, abilities, or attitudes, or note constantly changing trail conditions. The individual rider must use his or her own judgment as to where, when, and under what circumstances he or she will be able to ride; not only to assure their own safety but the safety of other trail users as well, and to assure the continued preservation of our public lands.

Be aware that mountain biking is a potentially strenuous activity with inherent risks and dangers. Hazards, whether natural or man made, whether mentioned within this text or not, can present themselves at any moment and under a vast array of unusual situations, or may occur where one did not previously. *Ride at your own risk!*

Although most routes are on public lands, some trails cross parcels of private property en route to, in the middle of, or exiting from these public lands. It is illegal to trespass upon private property whether posted or not. Civil action for damage to property can be maintained in the event of a trespass. Thus, it is the reader/rider's responsibility to obtain permission from land owners before crossing private property. Always respect the wishes and rights of a land owner and obey all posted signs restricting and regulating trail use. Also, realize that access to any route may change without notice. Mention of private property in this text is solely to identify changing land status. The author, in addition to any sponsor, group, or organization, assumes no liability in the event of trespass, accident, injury, or any action brought against any bicyclist or other trail user traveling any route mentioned in this book.

Finally, when on or off your bike, riding, hiking, or camping, abide by the "Code of Ethics" of backcountry travel. Remember, you are an ambassador for the promotion and preservation of the privilege to bicycle off the paved strip.

HOW FORTUNATE WE ARE to live so close to the mountains, to have an expansive playground only minutes from our doorsteps. With this luxury comes the problem of overcrowding and overuse. Can the central Wasatch Mountains continue to provide the recreational opportunities we have come to expect from them? Or are we simply eroding and destroying our beautiful and natural surroundings we so often take for granted?

Along the Wasatch Mountains there exist many hiking trails, or single tracks, that epitomize ATB travel. The terrain challenges the skills of beginner to advanced riders, producing the joy and exhilaration associated with off-road bicycling. Yet, many trails show signs off overcrowding. What are easy, popular hiking routes are now becoming the more frequented bicycling routes. In particular, the Salt Lake County Tri-Canyon area (Mill Creek Canyon and Big and Little Cottonwood canyons) has shown the most dramatic increase in users and may be considered the "hot spot" of trail use controversy—understandable since these routes are conveniently located adjacent to the metro area and host some of the most spectacular terrain along the Front. Tread lightly, venture into the sensitive and delicate areas sparingly, explore new terrain that might better withstand the assault of human impact, and use but don't abuse this remarkable and nonrenewable resource we call our backyard. The manner in which we ride will determine future trail policies, so keep the reputation of mountain bicyclists high in the eyes of all other trail users.

The main focus here is to make known the present situation so that each may carefully consider where and when to ride to assure the continued privilege to do so. Keep your eyes and ears open, voice your opinion, and become involved with groups and organizations that regulate and maintain trails crossing our public lands. A passive attitude is the worst attitude. Let's keep multi-use trails exactly that, available to all.

Skyline Trail
to Ben Lomond Peak

Trail Number:	W-1
Location:	North Ogden Pass.
Access:	North on I-15, exit #352 (North Ogden). Drive east on S.R. 134 1 mile to the stop sign, right (south) on S.R. 89 (1000 West), left immediately on S.R. 235 (2550 North), then left (north) on 400 East (Washington Boulevard) at Smith's. Turn right (east) on 2600 North following a sign for North Ogden Pass, left (north) after 1 mile onto 1050 East, right (east) after 0.7 mile on 3100 North for North Ogden Drive, then 3.1 miles up the canyon to a U.S.F.S. sign at the Divide. If you know a more direct route, take it.
Parking:	Provided at North Ogden Divide.
Trailhead:	On the north side of the road opposite the parking lot at a posted U.S.F.S. multi-use trail sign.
Type:	Out and back, single track.
Land Status:	U.S.F.S.
Maps:	U.S.G.S. 7.5' Quad.: North Ogden, Utah.
Length/Time:	6.6 mi./2 hr. (one way to Ben Lomond Peak). Allow 45 minutes to 1 hour for the return ride.
Elevation Changes:	
High:	8,700' (base of Ben Lomond Peak)
Low:	6,184' (trailhead)
Change:	2,516'
Overall Difficulty:	Difficult.
Technical Difficulty:	Moderate/technical.

APPROXIMATELY HALF THE ELEVATION is gained in the first 2.5 miles up a series of rocky, exposed, narrow switchbacks. Once on the ridge, this trail typifies other ridge trails with a sequence of short, moderate to difficult ascents and descents over small ridge-top peaks along an often exposed trail. This ride offers incredible views of the Wasatch Faultline and of the Great Salt Lake.

(Note: The Skyline Trail is a multi-use trail open to hikers, equestrians, bicycles, and motorcycles.)

Description

Allowing little time to warm up, this ride begins with a 1,200 foot climb over 2.4 miles, up ten distinct switchbacks, the first three of which resemble the Big Water Trail in Upper Mill Creek Canyon—a smooth, wide, single track rising gently through trees and thick brush. Past switchbacks three and four, the trail steepens and is moderately technical. Through switchbacks six to ten, the ascent becomes difficult and technical—rocks are numerous, turns are extremely sharp, and the trail is very exposed.

Atop the switchbacks (m 2.4), the path climbs steadily up the back (east side) of the ridge for 1.8 miles before wrapping around to the front (west side) at a switchback that is quite obscure on the return descent (m 4.2); be aware of its location and use caution on the way down.

Approaching Chilly Peak, the smooth track climbs gently then flattens along a stretch locals call "Gravity Hill," a well deserved break with an opportunity to exercise those neglected higher gears.

From the saddle just north of Chilly Peak (m 5.0) the view is dynamic: To the south across the divide, Lewis Peak attests to why the Wasatch Front is considered one of the steepest mountain ranges in the United States—an impervious rock wall uplifted along a razor sharp faultline, to the north looms Ben Lomond Peak, a conglomeration of folded and faulted Cambrian shale and limestone layers capped with a wedge of older Cambrian Tintic Quartzite thrusted up from great depth. Also passing through this saddle is a faultline. Contrast the gray and white limestone beds forming the cliffs of Chilly Peak to the south with the gray to black shales and tan quartzites immediately to the north along the trail.

Continue along the ridge up a short, very steep, but technically minimal hill called "The Wall" (there's only one excuse for not riding this hill, wimp) then to the base of Ben Lomond Peak at an old weather-beaten wooden trail map (m 6.6). Although the trail continues up to the summit of Ben Lomond, those who have attempted this ascent claim it to be 90 percent rideable for experts, 50-75 percent rideable for advanced riders, and a better hike than bike for intermediates.

Descending from Ben Lomond on the Skyline Trail.

The ride back down is fast, fun, and what mountain biking is all about. But be cautious as the descent requires total concentration and keen riding skills, and be prepared for a rough, jarring ride down the upper set of switchbacks.

Areas worth exploring: The following were not ridden but were brought to my attention by the local Ogden bicycling contingent. Both are for experienced riders.

Option W-1.1:   Cold Canyon.

From the base of Ben Lomond Peak at the rustic wooden trail sign (**m 6.6**), head east down Cold Canyon. The correct trail descends due east into the pines, immediately over a small wooden bridge by a spring, and past an old cabin/foundation. Do not confuse this route with a horse trail heading northeast through the fence line from the wooden trail sign.

This option drops into Ogden Valley along the North Fork of the Ogden River and requires either a car shuttle or a long grind on paved road back up to the Divide.

Option W-1.2:   Skyline Trail to Lewis Peak.

From the parking lot a multi-use trail heads south, climbing the ridgeline toward Lewis Peak. This trail is much more difficult than the ascent to Ben Lomond, as it climbs 2,000 feet in about 2.0 miles. Once on the ridge, a trail descends the eastern flank of the range dropping into the Eden-Huntsville area. Again, a car shuttle back to the Divide is advantageous. Inquire locally before attempting either of these options.

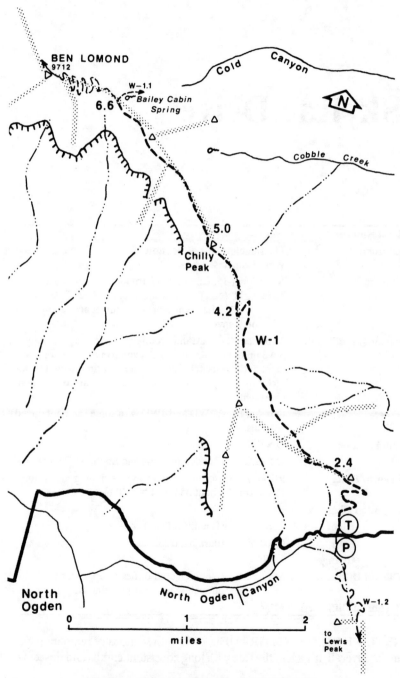

Skyline Trail to Ben Lomond Peak.

Skyline Drive

Trail Number:	W-2
Location:	The ridgeline east of Bountiful between Farmington and Ward Canyons.
Access:	North on I-15, exit #325 (Farmington, Lagoon Drive). Turn right (east) on State Street (S.R. 227) then left (north) on 100 East which provides direct access into Farmington Canyon.
Parking/Trailhead:	At or near Sunset Campground (U.S.F.S.), approximately 4.3 miles up Farmington Canyon from the end of pavement at the Wasatch-Cache National Forest sign. Do not block or park in campsites unless you plan to use them overnight.
Type:	Out and back, 2WD and 4WD with some remnant paved sections.
Land Status:	U.S.F.S.
Maps:	U.S.G.S. 7.5' Quads.: Peterson and Bountiful Peak, Utah.
Length/Time:	9.8 mi./1 hr. 45 min. (one way). Including all options, round trip is about 35 mi./4 hrs. 30 min.
Elevation Changes:	

High:	9,260'	(Bountiful Peak)
Low:	6,400'	(parking/trailhead)
Change:	2,860'	
Overall Difficult:	Moderate.	(Note: Overall difficulty upgrades to difficult when incorporating all options.)
Technical Difficulty:	Minor.	

SKYLINE DRIVE IS A GRADED 2WD with sections of remnant pavement. Overall, it's a lengthy ride with long consistent climbs and descents.

Options include 2WD and 4WD of minor to moderate technical difficulty. From atop Bountiful Peak is perhaps the best panorama of the Great Salt Lake with a distant view of the central Wasatch, Tri-Canyon peaks east of Salt Lake City.

Description

Both Farmington and Ward Canyons, accessing the Bountiful/Francis Peak ridgeline and Skyline Drive, are long, steep, consistent grades on maintained but washboard 2WD dirt and gravel roads. Since the beauty of this ride is along the high ridgeline, gain most of this mundane elevation by vehicle. Of course, heartier souls may start pedalling at the base of either canyon, but should anticipate a grueling 5,000 foot climb.

The most striking difference between this ride and other Wasatch rides is in the geology. No longer are you passing through prehistoric time while crossing distinct boundaries of the prominent, tilted Paleozoic sedimentary strata of Big and Little Cottonwood Canyons. Instead, this ride ventures up canyons and onto ridges exposing the much older Precambrian metamorphic rocks (greater than 1.5 billion years old) formed long before the layered sedimentary units common to the Salt Lake County Tri-Canyon Area.

Here, the Farmington Complex (aptly named) consists of rock types like schist, amphibolite, gneiss, and migmatite. All signify metamorphic rocks—rocks formed or altered by the intense heat and pressure produced within the Earth's crust. Typically, the result is twisted and contorted rock with alternating dark and light layers, much like that of a marble cake. Upon close examination, you'll notice white or pink ribbons of varying widths (called pegmatites and composed mainly of the light colored minerals quartz and feldspar) cutting across the predominant banding (foliation). These once fluid, molten masses were injected into the surrounding rock along faults, fractures, or other zones of weakness. When riding up Farmington Canyon look for contrasts in how these rocks have been crunched, bent, and compressed into sometimes small, tight, fist size folds.

Starting at the Sunset Campground, the Farmington Canyon Road rises gently 2.8 miles to the junction with the Francis Peak access road, marked by a huge, red steel gate (Option W-2.2).

Switch back to the right (west) up a moderately difficult but technically minor section to the junction with the Farmington Flats Road and Bountiful Peak Campground (m 3.4, Option W-2.1).

Turn right (west) again, past the group reservation campground, and wind uphill to Farmington Lake. A 0.2 mile dirt foot trail heading to the

**Contorted metamorphic rocks of the
Farmington Complex.**

lake (forking west from this sharp left-handed switchback) is rideable only in part, but well worth the hike. Skyline Drive continues uphill past several spurs leading to summer homes (all are to be respected as private property) and onto the ridgeline 450 feet above the lake. Even though the ascent is steep, most of the road is paved, thus providing excellent traction.

Proceed south climbing steadily to Bountiful Peak (**m 7.4**). From the small ridge extending to the west is the most outstanding perspective of the Great Salt Lake. On a clear day the view extends well beyond the lake to the mountains of eastern Nevada, while below, Antelope Island is completely engulfed by placid blue-green waters. Only from this vantage point

Serenity awaits at Farmington Lake.

can you appreciate the immense size of this land-locked body of water, the remains of the ancient and even larger Lake Bonneville.

About 2.0 miles south and downhill from Bountiful Peak (**m 9.4**), a rustic 4WD branches right (northwest) through what was once the Parrish Creek Research Center. To ride the full 1.5 mile loop (the only real off-road riding on this trip—moderately technical), turn right (downhill) at a prominent, tight, left hand switchback about 0.3 mile from Skyline Drive. Three small water crossings add to this option before exiting back onto the main road. Although tempting to coast further down Skyline Drive to the south, remember that more effortless downhill cruising translates to more grueling uphill upon returning.

Return the exact opposite way, but be aware that the descent from Bountiful Peak is potentially very fast; use extreme caution when rounding corners and watch for sections where the pavement has been eroded away, exposing loose dirt and gravel beneath.

Option W-2.1:   Farmington Flats (loop, 4WD, 4.6 mi./30 min., 160', easy, minor).

Back at the group reservation area (**m 3.4**), turn right (south) toward Bountiful Peak Campground and the Farmington Guard Station. Rising only 160 feet in elevation, this enjoyable and relaxing loop passes through evergreen and aspen, across brush covered fields, and is an easy alternative for those not inclined to climb up onto the ridgeline. 3.7 miles along the loop, the road exits onto the Francis Peak access road at a large white maintenance building. Turn left (south) to descend into Farmington Canyon; turn right (north) to ascend Francis Peak.

Option W-2.2:   Francis Peak Road (out and back, 2WD, 5.0 mi./50 min. one way to Francis Peak, 2,000', moderate/difficult, minor).

Starting at the red gate at the top of Farmington Canyon, this road climbs steadily with few breaks to the radar facility (private property) atop Francis Peak (elev. 9,547')—a long, long grind on a well maintained graded dirt and gravel road. A mile or so past Francis Peak sit Smith Creek Lakes on the east side of the ridge.

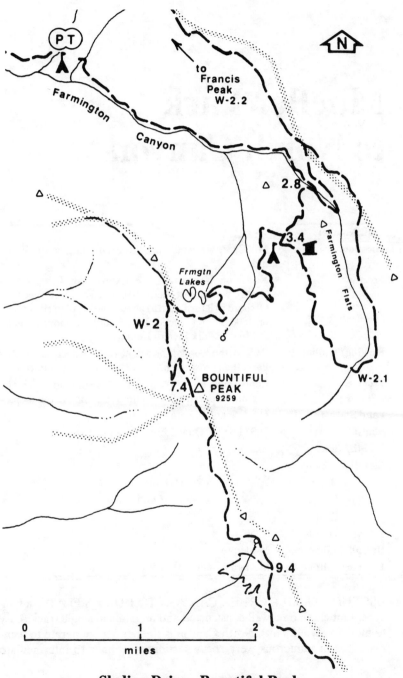

Skyline Drive—Bountiful Peak

Mueller Park
to North Canyon

Trail Number:	W-3
Location:	Mill Creek (Mueller Park Picnic Ground), east of Bountiful.
Access:	North on I-15, exit #318 (North Salt Lake/Woods Cross). Travel east then north on 2600 South (becomes Orchard as it turns north) about 2 miles, then right (east) on 1800 South (Mueller Park Road) for about 2.4 miles to Mueller Park Picnic Grounds.
Parking/Trailhead:	Park at the wooden bridge at the entrance to Mueller Park, then cross the bridge (south) onto the dirt trail.
Type:	Loop, single track, 4WD (at the base of North Canyon), and minor paved road required to complete the loop.
Land Status:	U.S.F.S. and private property.
Maps:	U.S.G.S. 7.5' Quad.: Fort Douglas, Utah.
Length/Time:	13.5 mi./2 hr. 45 min.

Elevation Changes:

High:	7,160'	(Rudy's Flat)
Low:	5,000'	(mouth of Mill Creek)
Change:	2,160'	
Trailhead	5,250'	

Overall Difficulty:	Moderate.
Technical Difficulty:	Moderate.

ASCENDING MILL CREEK CANYON TO RUDY'S FLAT is a long consistent climb on a well constructed and maintained single track (easy to moderately difficult). North Canyon is steeper and moderate to technical due to numerous, very rocky sections. Beginner to intermediate

High above the Salt Lake Valley near Rudy's Flat.

riders will find it easier to ascend Mill Creek, whereas advanced riders may enjoy ascending North Canyon. Numerous locations afford views of the Great Salt Lake Valley. The enjoyment to be found on this trail rivals that of the Bigwater Trail to Dog Lake.

(Note: This multi-use trail is open to hikers, equestrians, bicycles, and motorcycles.)

Description

Cross the bridge at the entrance to Mueller Park onto the single track climbing the southern slopes of Mill Creek. Initially, the trail passes through aspen and fir, but grades into scrub oak with elevation. The first 3.5 miles to Big Rock (a Precambrian pegmatite plug) is easy to moderately difficult with minor technical difficulty except for occasional slightly rocky stretches.

At Big Rock, the trail switches back to the south and becomes slightly steeper, winding its way up through low lying brush, quaking aspen, then fir trees approaching Rudy's Flat (**m 6.5**, private property), the most enjoyable section. The area abounds with blooming flowers and wildlife; deer are common.

Rudy's Flat is marked by a small meadow surrounded by a few tall pines, a tranquil setting to relax in before descending.

As the trail heads west out of Rudy's Flat it passes through a small saddle and begins down North Canyon. This upper section is loaded with loose sharp rocks and is quite technical—an easy place to puncture a tire.

Contouring the southern slopes of North Canyon, the single track switches back several times, crosses the creek twice, then exits onto a 4WD in the bottom of the canyon (**m 8.9**). Although the past 2.4 mile descent from Rudy's Flat is not all that difficult, beware of many rocky stretches in the trail just when you least expect them.

Paralleling the creek, the 4WD (hardly passable in 4WD though) is often very deeply rutted and contains abundant imbedded rocks toward the bottom; it is a bone jarring ride. After 1.3 miles, the 4WD exits onto Canyon Creek Road (**m 10.2**). Ride down the paved road for 0.8 mile, turn right (north) on Bountiful Boulevard and ride past the golf course (another good reason to wear a helmet!), and complete the journey by turning right (east) on Mueller Park Road and back to the parking area.

(Note: As with any loop, this trail may be ridden in either direction. Mill Creek from Mueller Park offers a more gentle ascent to Rudy's Flat, consequently a smoother descent. North Canyon is much more difficult and technical to ascend, thus a rocky, bumpy ride down.)

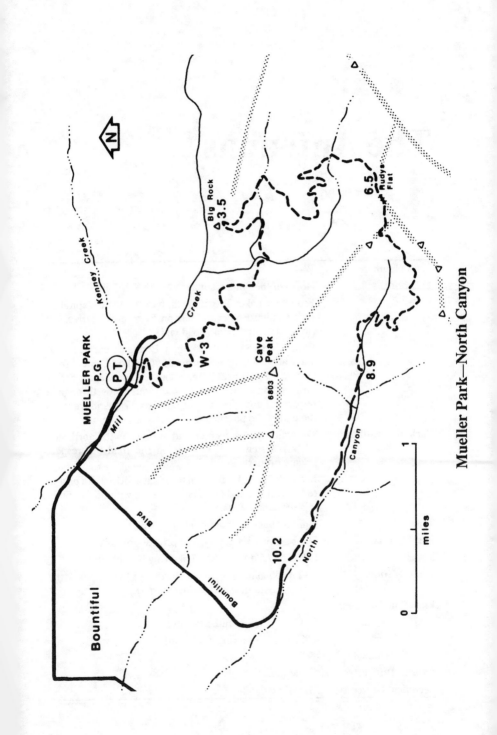

Mueller Park—North Canyon

The Antennas

Trail Number:	W-4
Location:	North of the State Capital to North Salt Lake.
Access:	From Salt Lake: Travel north, past the State Capital on East Capital Boulevard, left on Edgecombe Drive, left (west) on Dorchester (dead end).
	From North Salt Lake: Follow Beck's Street (S.R. 89) north about 4 miles and turn right (east) on Center Street in North Salt Lake. After about 1 mile, Center Street turns directly into Lacey Way and winds through a residential area. Turn right on Gary Way and travel to the end of the pavement.
Parking/Trailhead:	The trail begins at a green and red gate on the north side of Dorchester. Park here or on the road but respect private property as this is a residential area.
	In North Salt Lake, the trail begins at a locked and posted red gate at the end of Gary Way. Park with discretion in this residential area.
Type:	Out and back with optional loop, 4WD.
Land Status:	U.S.F.S., Salt Lake City, and private property.
Maps:	U.S.G.S. 7.5' Quad.: Salt Lake City North, Utah.
Length/Time:	4.3 mi./30 min. (one way to North Salt Lake). Allow the same amount of time for the return trip.
Elevation Changes:	
High:	5,610' (first radio facility)
Low:	4,920' (parking/trailhead)
Change:	690'
Overall Difficulty:	Moderate.
Technical Difficulty:	Minor/moderate.

THIS MAINTAINED 2WD ROAD provides access to the radio facilities (private property) above Ensign Peak and serves as a firebreak road. Climbing to the radio facility, from either direction, is moderate/difficult but of only minor/moderate technical difficulty, whereas the flat section into North Salt Lake is an easy cruise. From atop the radio facilities and City Creek Peak, outstanding views of the Salt Lake Valley to the south and the "scenic" oil refineries to the west dominate. The Antennas ride is one of the best late evening sunset rides.

(Note: As posted by the Salt Lake City Watershed Management, this road is closed to all unauthorized motorized vehicles.)

Description

Initially heading west, the road soon turns north past the base of Ensign Peak then begins to climb steadily with the steepest section about 0.3 mile from the first radio facility (**m 1.7**). Primarily dirt and gravel, the road offers good traction.

At the radio towers, the road splits. To the right, it climbs to the second radio facility (Option W-4.1); however, the main trail continues north descending into Jones Canyon (a short, difficult, moderately technical climb upon returning), wraps around the base of Meridian Peak, then travels northeast along the ancient shoreline of Lake Bonneville, the huge ancestor to the present Great Salt Lake. This 2.0 mile stretch is flat and an easy roller coaster ride until it crosses a north-south gravel road (**m 4.3**) accessing Gary Way (paved).

Although the 4WD dirt road continues across the gravel road, it enters upon private property and is clearly posted. In the past bicycling around the gravel pit has been allowed with the land owner's permission, but an incident where trail users have torn down the "No Trespassing" signs and cut fences has changed the owner's views. More succinctly, do not ride around the back side of the gravel pit without permission.

(Note: Although tempting, do not venture into the gravel pit. This is private property where heavy machinery and large dump trucks operate.)

Option W-4.1:   Meridian Peak (loop, 4WD, 4.2 mi./1 hr., difficult, technical—for advanced riders).

From the first radio tower, follow the 4WD branching east and uphill toward the second radio facility (a steep, difficult, moderate/technical climb with abundant loose rocks), but stay to the right as this route bypasses the towers and continues climbing to City Creek Peak (**m 1.3**). The view from City Creek Peak is awe-inspiring as the Salt Lake Valley below

Late evening sun casts long shadows across City Creek Canyon.

stretches south to Point of the Mountain. Mt. Olympus dominates the forefront, while the Cottonwood Twin Peaks and Lone Peak cap the jagged Wasatch skyline.

Turning north, the 4WD follows the ridgeline west of City Creek Canyon and becomes quite rocky and eventually unrideable. About half a mile northeast of City Creek Peak, turn left along a 4WD heading west out onto a low ridge. Shortly thereafter, the path descends sharply to the southwest, then climbs very steeply to the top of Meridian Peak (yes, this climb is rideable if you avoid the abundant loose rocks in the trail). Appropriately named, Meridian Peak (**m 2.5**) falls in line with the Salt Lake Meridian paralleling Main Street, splitting the city between east and west.

Descending Meridian Peak is very difficult and very technical (i.e., *mucho* rocks). Start by making sure your helmet is securely fastened, then head southwest into a small saddle. Even though the trail appears to climb back up another hill directly south and in front of you, descend to the west out of the saddle along a vague, rutted, pseudo-4WD trail. Follow this bone-jarring path west as it drops (literally) and connects with Bonneville Drive below. Turn left following Bonneville Drive back to the first radio facility to complete the loop (a moderate/difficult climb).

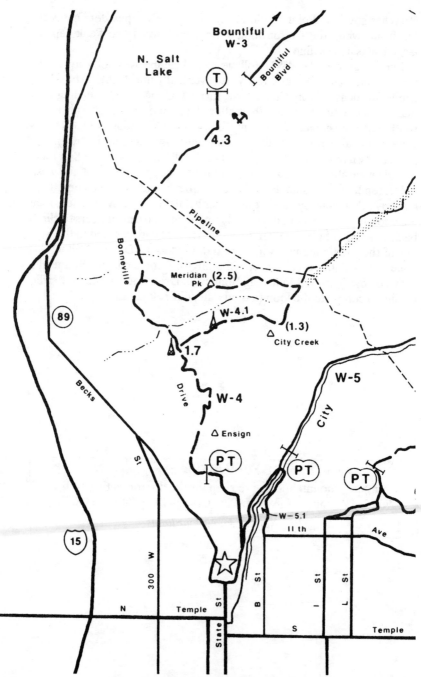

**The Antennas, City Creek Canyon,
and Avenues Twin Peaks**

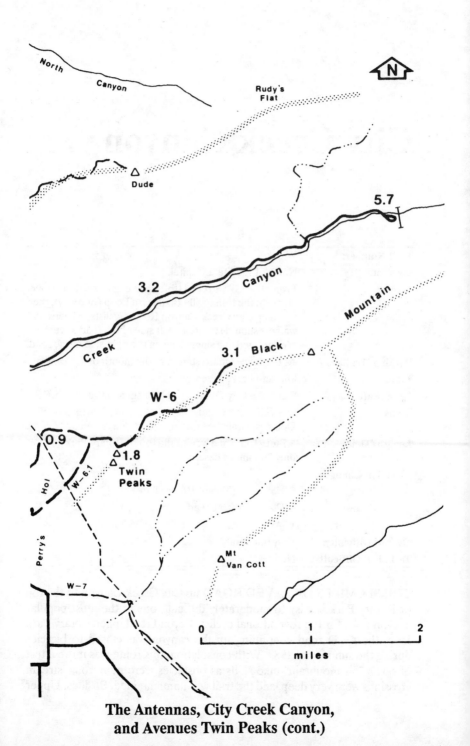

**The Antennas, City Creek Canyon,
and Avenues Twin Peaks (cont.)**

City Creek Canyon

Trail Number:	W-5
Location:	North of the State Capital.
Access:	From the "B" Street-11th Avenue intersection, travel north on the Bonneville Boulevard Loop (one way), then north up City Creek Canyon Road. Cyclists, joggers, and walkers should stay to the left side of the road as vehicles are confined to a single lane on the right side of the road.
Parking/Trailhead:	At the fence/guard station at the mouth of the canyon.
Type:	Out and back, paved.
Land Status:	Salt Lake City (Watershed Management) and U.S.F.S.
Maps:	U.S.G.S. 7.5' Quads: Salt Lake City, North and Fort Douglas, Utah. See trail map for "The Antennas" (W-4).
Length/Time:	5.7 mi./1 hr. (one way-to the top of Rotary Park). Allow only 30 min. to descend.
Elevation Changes:	
High:	6,045' (Top of Rotary Park)
Low:	4,700' (trailhead)
Change:	1,345'
Overall Difficulty:	Easy/moderate.
Technical Difficulty:	None.

THE SIX MILES OF PAVED ROAD up City Creek Canyon to the top of Rotary Park is easy to moderately difficult, one of the most popular canyon rides for the recreational cyclist. Beyond the Upper Rotary Park loop, the 4WD road continuing up the canyon was closed to bicycles during the summer of 1988. With consolation, this route was more a test of one's "dis-mountain" bike skills as obstacles were numerous, stream crossings were very deep, and the trail was unmaintained. Besides, Upper

Popular with walkers, joggers, and bicyclists, City Creek Canyon is only minutes from downtown Salt Lake City.

City Creek Canyon is managed as a Wilderness Area. Memory Grove, at the mouth of City Creek Canyon, is an easy two mile loop directly accessible from the city's central business district.

(Note: See the chapter "Land Ownership" for rules and regulations for recreational canyon use.)

Description

Park at the mouth of the canyon and squeeze through the gap in the fence line next to the guard station (don't bother trying to ride through). For 5.7 miles the narrow paved road parallels the thickly forested canyon drainage below rounded barren hills.

Past the water treatment plant (**m 3.2**), the paved road narrows to a single lane and steepens slightly approaching Rotary Park; the loop marks the top of the paved canyon road. Vegetation thickens and air cools as you rise in elevation. Relax on a picnic table next to the rushing stream before preparing for one of the most enjoyable downhill glides along the Wasatch Front.

(Note: Since City Creek is very popular with walkers, joggers, and bicyclists, please adhere to standard bicycling regulations: stay far to the right and ride in single file. Many of the corners in the canyon, especially near the top, are sharp and blind. Here, more than anywhere, you should anticipate someone around the next corner, as is usually the case.)

Option W-5.1:   Memory Grove (loop, paved road and dirt foot path, 2.0 mi./15 min., easy).

Head south out of City Creek Canyon, across Bonneville Boulevard, past a few rock barriers, and on to a narrow, single lane, paved road (closed to motor vehicles). About 0.5 mile down the paved lane, cross a wooden bridge to the left, then turn right descending on a dirt foot path. Used extensively by walkers, hikers, and picnickers, this path parallels the creek and passes a series of monuments and plaques honoring war veterans and pioneers of western exploration. Enveloped in the lush canyon vegetation, the trail offers a peaceful retreat only minutes away from the city's central business district. Exit the trail at the Veteran's Memorial Monument and loop north back up the paved road to the parking area in City Creek Canyon.

GASTRONOMY, INC.

gastronomy (gas • `trän • ə • mē): 1. the art of good eating
Market Street Grill & Oyster Bar ■ 60 Post Office Place ■ SLC

Protect our watersheds—camp away from water sources

Avenues' Twin Peaks

Trail Number:	W-6
Location:	Above the Avenues.
Access:	Head north on "L" Street, right (northeast) on Northcliff Drive, then left (north) on Terrace Hills Drive to the end of the road.
Parking/Trailhead:	Use discretion when parking at the top of Terrace Hills Drive (dead end), a residential area.
Type:	Out and back, 4WD.
Land Status:	U.S.F.S., Salt Lake City, and private property.
Maps:	U.S.G.S. 7.5' Quad.: Fort Douglas, Utah. See trail map for "The Antennas" (W-4).
Length/Time:	3.1 mi./45 min. (one way to the base of Black Mountain). Allow 30 min. for the return ride.
Elevation Changes:	
High:	6,600' (base of Black Mountain)
Low:	5,300' (trailhead)
Change:	1,300'
Overall Difficulty:	Difficult.
Technical Difficulty:	Moderate/technical.

A SO CALLED JEEP ROAD, the trail to Twin Peaks and Black Mountain contains numerous short, very steep, and often very rocky hills requiring much pushing depending on your riding skills and overall strength. But, anything for a great view, right? Wildflowers abound in the springtime.

Description

Of the three trails extending from the end of Terrace Hills Drive, the 4WD to the right (blocked by a large brown gate and posted "No Motor Vehicles...") heading east into scrub oak is the correct way. This often deeply eroded and rutted 4WD winds up the south side of Valleyview Canyon 0.9 mile to a saddle above City Creek Canyon to the west—a moderately difficult climb.

Through the saddle passes a pipeline trail which drops into City Creek Canyon but has since been closed to all vehicles (bikes included). With consolation, this descent into City Creek is dangerously steep and very difficult to navigate.

To the northeast the trail appears to rise up an ominous hill; however, ride the single track that contours the hill more gently on its east side (may still require a good push).

**From behind the Capital and above the Avenues,
the Salt Lake Valley stretches out below.**

Once on the ridge, the 4WD heads east toward Twin Peaks over several smaller hills. Surmounting Twin Peaks is a near impossible ride and even a great struggle to push (**m 1.8**).

Continuing northeast, the trail follows the ridge approaching the base of Black Mountain—a difficult, technical stretch due to subsurface rock outcropping in the trail and more short, steep pitches requiring a fair share of dismounting and pushing. (Note: The trail crosses a small parcel of private property along this ridge.) As difficult and frustrating as this ride is, a staggering view of the Salt Lake Valley along with vibrant wildflowers coating the hillside keep everything in perspective. About 1.3 miles from Twin Peaks the trail ascending Black Mountain becomes too steep (**m 3.1**), but hiking up to the peak is a possible option.

Of course, never overlook the local geology. It is the subsurface conglomerate (a rock consisting of numerous rounded pebble to cobble size clasts cemented in a finer sandy matrix, indicative of transport and deposition by very fast flowing waters, i.e., rivers) that makes this trail so technical and arduous. When eroded, this rock produces all the pebbles, cobbles, and boulders strewn across the trail.

More interesting are the fins and parallel vertical ridges on the northeast facing slopes of Upper City Creek Canyon. Like ribs on a skeleton, these ridges are a sequence of Cambrian to Pennsylvanian age sandstones and limestones (west to east, respectively) uprighted and overturned by local folding of the earth's crust. Shadows cast by the late evening sun accentuate each individual fin.

Option W-6.1:   Perry's Hollow (portions on private property).

Instead of returning along the same route down Valleyview Canyon, turn left (south) on a small ridge just to the west of Twin Peaks. Moderately difficult and again somewhat rocky, this vague, 4WD drops into Perry's Hollow. At the bottom of the hollow in the thick brush, noted by a rubbish pile and an old, tattered, blue couch, turn right along a path that switches back immediately and crosses over to the west side of the drainage. Finally, this dirt road exits through a newly developed residential area onto paved Bonneville Boulevard. Head northwest on Bonneville Boulevard, then turn right on Terrace Hills Drive and up a short grunt back to the trailhead.

The "U" Trail

Trail Number:	W-7
Location:	Behind (east of) the University of Utah.
Access/Parking/	
Trailhead:	There are two main access points to the trail:
	1) Northwest: Virginia Street Park—behind Shriner's Hospital at the corner of Virginia Street (1340 East) and 11th Avenue (360 North),
	2) Mid Trail: Behind Ft. Douglas at the entrance to Red Butte Canyon and the State Arboretum,
	Access to this trail may be gained from many more locations in addition to the ones noted.
Type:	Out and back, 4WD.
Land Status:	U.S.F.S., Salt Lake City, University of Utah, and private property.
Maps:	U.S.G.S. 7.5' Quad.: Fort Douglas, Utah.
Length/Time:	3.7 mi./40 min. (one way). Allow the same amount of time for the return trip.

Elevation Changes:		
High:	5,200'	(fence line above Pioneer Trail State Park)
Low:	4,840'	(Virginia Street Park trailhead)
Change:	360'	
Overall Difficulty:	Easy/moderate.	
Technical Difficulty:	Minor/moderate.	

EXCEPT FOR A FEW SHORT moderate to difficult hills, the ride is essentially flat, brief, and technically minor, a good ride for the beginner. Also, due to its proximity to the metropolitan area, it's a great ride for those who have only a few hours to play. The short optional ascent of Soldier's Hollow is only moderately difficult.

Description

At the intersection of Virginia Street and 11th Avenue, the trail follows a 4WD pipeline maintenance road east behind Shriner's Hospital. After a gentle **0.5** mile rise, a trail forks left (northeast) up to the white "U" on the hill. However, continue straight along the main road, past a large brown steel gate descending slightly into the mouth of Dry Creek.

Circle out of Dry Creek southeast along a smooth 2WD heading toward University Hospital. Just before the dirt road joins with paved (**m 1.1**), switch back to the north along a 4WD that parallels the previous 2WD dirt road but slightly uphill. After 0.2 mile, the 4WD turns east for a short, sustained, moderate to difficult climb.

Now the 4WD follows power lines southeast hugging the foothills and weaving in and out of small side gulches. During spring and early summer, sego lilies (the state flower of Utah) dot the hillside.

Soon, the trail heads into Battle Gulch (**m 1.7**) but is impossible to ride, as the southeast side of the gulch is a 20 to 30 foot wall that is even difficult to walk up. Instead, take the gravel road (short, but technical and steep) to the south before the gulch, then ascend a short steep hill on the south side of the gulch back up onto the main trail. Thereafter, the trail proceeds a short distance before dropping into the mouth of Red Butte Canyon (**m 2.5**). Bicycles are prohibited up Red Butte Canyon, a wilderness study area.

Turn left toward the entrance to the State Arboretum (bicycles prohibited, again) but head southeast past the Arboretum's entrance gate on the continued 4WD trail. Again following the pipeline, the path rises gently, turns east, and ends at the fence line above Pioneer Trail State Park (**m 3.7**).

The dirt roads in the park below are part of Old Deseret, a reconstructed pioneer village representing the period from 1847 to 1869. Horsedrawn vehicles and pedestrians may be encountered here at any time. For their protection, bicycling on these roads is not encouraged. To wander through Old Deseret and "Feel and observe everyday life as it was lived in pioneer Utah," ride paved Foothill Boulevard from the Fort Douglas-University of Utah area to Sunnyside Avenue (2100 East and 800 South), head east on Sunnyside Avenue for about a mile to the park entrance, lock your bike near the Visitor's Center, then stroll along the village's dirt roads or ride in one of the horse drawn wagons.

Upon returning from the trail's end at the fence line above Pioneer

Can you name this trail?

Trail State Park, hug the foothills and bear right onto a single track that wraps in and out of George's Hollow and Soldier's Hollow then drops down to the Arboretum gate.

Option W-7.1: Soldier's Hollow (loop, 4WD, 1.0 mi./15 min., 400', moderate, moderate).

About 300 yards southeast of the Arboretum entrance gate along the pipeline road, a 4WD heads northeast paralleling the south side of Red Butte Canyon. The trail immediately passes an old, cement foundation then climbs for 0.5 mile up to a burned out sandstone building.

From the sandstone building drop down a short, steep hill (walking recommended), then head west along a single track back to the pipeline trail. Or, continue the climb up Soldier's Hollow to a small quarry 0.4 miles above.

The pale orange, cross-bedded sandstone in this quarry, and which the burned building is made of, is part of the Jurassic/Triassic Nugget Sandstone extending through Park City to the southern Uintas near Vernal. The Nugget Sandstone was deposited mostly as wind blown dunes, a co-relative of the well-known Navajo Sandstone in southern Utah. Utilized extensively as a building stone, it is popular in buildings and houses in the Avenues area, and most notably in the First Presbyterian Church on South Temple.

(Note: There are many more dirt roads through this area than the one mentioned here. Fortunately, all trend in the same general direction, providing the option of creating your own little loops. Construction of the Virginia Street Park behind Shriner's Hospital began in late 1988, altering the northwest trailhead. Sponsored by Salt Lake City, the park will continue to allow access to this trail, may actually improve it, and will provide more adequate parking.)

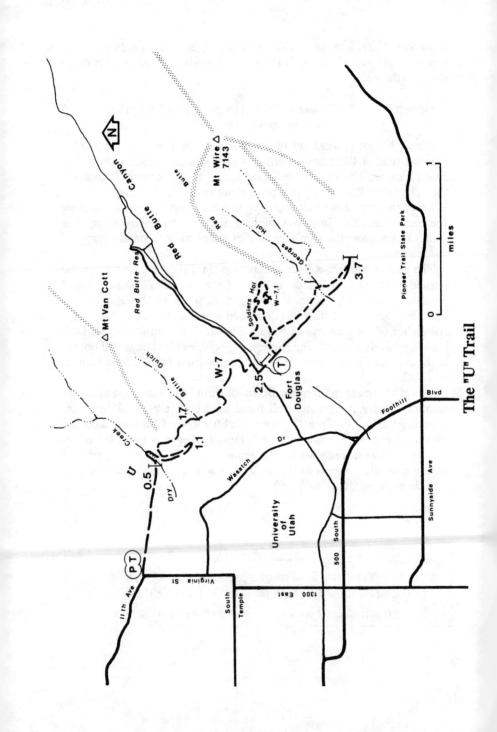

The "U" Trail

Little Mountain Summit/ Killyon Canyon

Trail Number:	W-8
Location:	Summit of Emigration Canyon Road.
Access:	From Foothill Boulevard (at about 2100 East), head east on Sunnyside Avenue (800 South), past Hogle Zoo, then approximately 7.5 miles up Emigration Canyon Road to Little Mountain Summit.
Parking:	At Little Mountain Summit, park on the south side of the road.
Trailhead:	Directly opposite the parking area on the north side of the road at a red steel gate.
Type:	Loop, 4WD, single track, and paved road.
Land Status:	U.S.F.S., Salt Lake City, private property.
Maps:	U.S.G.S. 7.5' Quad.: Mountain Dell, Utah.
Length/Time:	7.4 mi./1 hr. 20 min.
Elevation Changes:	

High:	6,900'	(near Birch Springs)
Low:	5,840'	(Emigration Canyon Road)
Change:	1,060'	
Trailhead:	6,230'	

Overall Difficulty:	Moderate/difficult.
Technical Difficulty:	Moderate/technical.

ALTHOUGH A SHORT RIDE, it contains half a dozen short, very steep ascents and descents along a narrow often overgrown single track with two minor water crossings. Passing through the heart of the burnzone of the 1988 Emigration Canyon wildfire, the contrast between black-charred

Splashing through the lower portion of Killyon Canyon.

trees, green grasses, and vivid wildflowers is striking. From high points on the trail, you are treated to beautiful vistas of the Mill Creek ridgeline marked by Grandeur Peak, Mount Aire, and Murdock Peak along with Mount Olympus and Gobbler's Knob capping the distant skyline. Without question, Emigration Canyon is one of the most popular canyons for jogging and bicycling, due to its proximity to the city and gentle grade. Combining the canyon ride with this off-road loop is an excellent 20-mile, all-afternoon affair.

Description

The trail begins at the red gate on the north side of the road opposite the parking area. This gate, along with a large earthen berm, close the trail to all motorized vehicles. Although the trailhead exists on U.S.F.S. land, the path soon passes over about one half mile of private property before continuing on public lands.

Without time to warm up, the ride begins with one of the steepest climbs encountered along its length and is an indication of what lies ahead—about six more similar hills. Fortunately, all are short like this first one, so walking is not too humbling. Surmounting this hill, the trail continues northeast along a 4WD that was bulldozed as a firebreak line for the Emigration Canyon wildfire during the summer of 1988, thus its condition was severely worsened—mainly poorly consolidated dirt with abundant debris. For all practical purposes this rough 4WD has now graded to a narrow single-track. After 1.0 mile, a second steep hill is encountered, shortly thereafter you face yet a third hill more intimidating than the first two. Fortunately, the trail splits here (**m 1.3**). Follow a rocky, technical single track branching to the right, passing into tall scrub oak, and circumnavigating around the hill to the east.

With the pounding of your heart ringing in your ears from these past few steep ascents, continue north through tall oaks (often enveloping the trail in a canopy of green) along a roller coaster ride over a series of still more short, steep ups and downs. Control your speed as the path is quite narrow. Shortly past Little Mountain the trail descends into an open meadow (where powerlines pass overhead), after which is encountered the hardest and final climb of the ride—the highest point on the trail. Descend north into another clearing at the head of Killyon Canyon marked by a faint four way trail intersection and a small, relic fire ring (**m 3.3**). The trail north continues to Lookout Peak (more of a push than a ride); the trail east descends to Affleck Park via Birch Springs along a bulldozed path. Turn left (west) and descend Killyon Canyon.

The trail down Killyon Canyon (an old 4WD, now a single track for all practical purposes) is often deeply rutted and moderate to technical. 1.5 miles down the canyon trail (**m 4.8**) and two minor water crossings later, the dirt trail exits onto a maintained gravel road followed shortly by paved road. At the intersection with Emigration Canyon Road (**m 5.7**), turn left and ride 1.7 miles up the paved road back to the parking area.

As a result of the canyon's wildfire, the terrain is especially fragile and subject to accelerated erosion. Only clean, smart cycling will assure the quick rejuvination of the vegetation.

(Note: Making this ride even more enjoyable are the three fine eating establishments in Emigration Canyon: Cromptons, Ruth's Diner, and the Santa Fe. All have outdoor patios, and none frown upon those wearing tattered cycling clothes. The Little Mountain/Killyon Canyon Trail crosses small portions of private property. Please, treat the land with the respect due its owners. Failure to do so may result in the posting of private property/no trespassing signs, thus terminating our privilege to ride.)

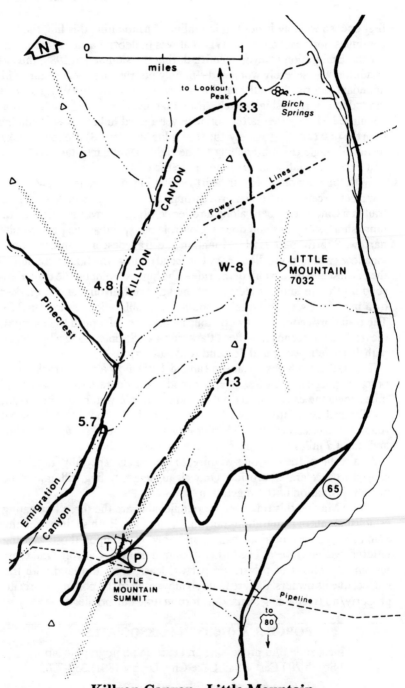

Killyon Canyon—Little Mountain

Big Water Trail to Dog Lake

Trail Number:	W-9
Location:	Upper Mill Creek Canyon.
Access:	Approximately 9.5 miles up Mill Creek Canyon Rd. (3800 South and about 3900 East) to the end of pavement.
Parking:	Two paved areas at the end of the road provide ample parking.
Trailhead:	Adjacent to the lower of the two parking areas, the path heads due west marked by a wooden trail sign.
Type:	Out and back, single track.
Land Status:	U.S.F.S.
Maps:	U.S.G.S. 7.5' Quad.: Mount Aire, Utah.
Length/Time:	3.2 mi., 45 min. (one way to Dog Lake). Allow 30 min. for the return trip.
Elevation Changes:	
High:	8,560' (ridge above Dog Lake)
Low:	7,600' (trailhead)
Change:	960'
Overall Difficulty:	Easy/moderate.
Technical Difficulty:	Minor/moderate.

THIS TRAIL CONSISTS OF A SERIES of short, moderately difficult climbs with long, flat stretches in between. Technical difficulty is minor except for occasional roots, log bars, and imbedded rocks. All drainages are covered with wooden foot bridges. Passing through very thick evergreens and aspens, this well constructed and maintained trail is the best (and by far the most popular) beginner/intermediate ride in the Wasatch Front. More importantly, the Big Water Trail is also one of the most popular multi-use trails among the central Wasatch, and is heavily traveled by hikers, equestrians, and other bicyclists. Unfortunately, solitude can rarely be found along this route as the number of users is enormous.

Description

Choose a low gear to begin this ride as the first few hundred yards is perhaps the most difficult section of the entire trail. Only a moderately difficult climb to the first switchback, the trail flattens then rises gently through thick evergreens and heavily vegetated slopes. Earthy hues of green and brown mixed with golden rays of sunlight bursting through the trees paint the trail.

After 1.0 mile, the path crosses its first drainage then switches back to the northeast. Over the next 2.0 miles the trail continues up a series of short, moderately difficult climbs offset by intermittent flats, winds in and out of small side drainages, crosses several wooden foot bridges, and switches back and forth up the lush hillsides.

About 2.7 miles up the trail, a distinct four way intersection (Little Water Trail) signifies the proximity of the top. Continue straight through this junction and immediately switchback to the right (southeast) for a short 0.2 mile rise to the summit (m 3.1) marked by a U.S.F.S. trail sign for the Desolation Trail. Dog Lake awaits at the bottom of the dirt/gravel trail to the left. Be cautious of the several log water bars (be sure to ride over them at right angles to prevent your wheels from sliding out from under you).

Dog Lake, like Lake Desolation, is a small alpine lake with no outlet.

Option W-9.1: Access to the Mount Olympus Wilderness boundary (out and back, single track, 0.7 mi./10 min. round trip, easy).

Ride around the west side of Dog Lake and onto the small ridge to the south. On the ridge, a vague path heads west (right) into the trees, rises steeply at first, then flattens as it approaches the Wilderness boundary sign 0.3 mile away. Upon returning, take the left fork which exits at the Desolation Trail sign above Dog Lake.

(Note: Presently, mountain bikes are prohibited from designated Wilderness Areas. The subject is one of debate but for the time being don't compound the issue, stay out! Violators can be fined. Ride into the wilderness areas now, and bicycles will never be allowed in the future.)

When descending the Big Water Trail use extreme caution, not that

The most popular mountain bike ride in the Wasatch.

the trail is technical, but that it is heavily traveled. Always anticipate some-one around the next corner: hikers both young and old, dogs, equestrians, and of course other cyclists. Since these trail users may not be watching out for you, you had better watch out for them.

Option W-9.2:   Lake Desolation from Dog Lake (out and back, single track, 2.3 mi./30 min. one way, 1,000', moderate/difficult, moderate/technical).

As the saying goes, "Look before you leap." Head east from Dog Lake down a steep **0.5** mile hill to the signed junction for Big Cottonwood Road (via Mill D) and Lake Desolation. This route is generally loose gravel with numerous off angle log water bars which are tricky to negotiate safe-ly. Ride slowly to prevent wheel lock up and erosion.

From the junction, the Desolation Trail branches left (east) and soon becomes a very steep, rugged, but short, climb. Afterward, the trail pas-ses through lush open meadows, up a few small rises, and across many more log bars. Past the meadows, another long difficult climb brings you to Lake Desolation (**m 2.4**).

Tranquil and isolated, Lake Desolation lies tucked beneath the Wasatch ridgeline among verdant Engleman spruce and Subalpine fir. From here options include pushing 400' up to the Wasatch Crest Trail then descending through upper Mill Creek Canyon, or dropping down Mill D Canyon to the Big Cottonwood Canyon Road, but it's a long way around to Mill Creek Canyon without a car shuttle. If returning via Dog Lake, be prepared to push the majority of the hill from the Desolation Trail/Mill D junction to Dog Lake.

(Note: The descent on the Mill D trail is described in Option W-11.1 of the Wasatch Crest Trail.)

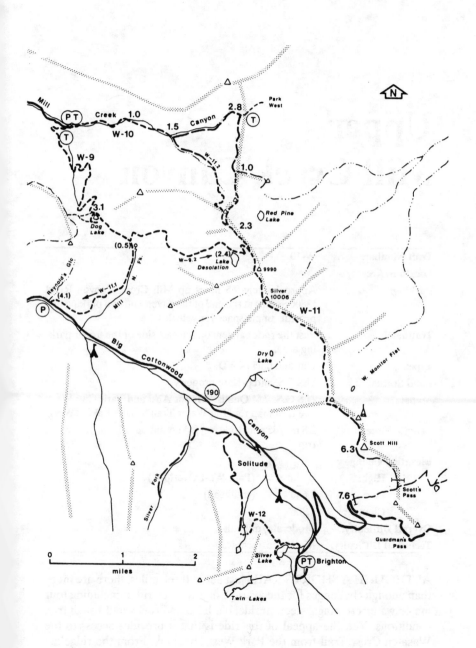

Upper Mill Creek and Big Cottonwood canyons

Upper Mill Creek Canyon

Trail Number:	W-10
Location/Access/	
Parking:	Approximately 9.5 miles up Mill Creek Canyon Road (3800 South) at the end of the pavement, two parking lots provide ample space for vehicles.
Trailhead:	Past the rock barriers on the east side of the upper parking area.
Type:	Out and back, 4WD.
Land Status:	U.S.F.S. and private property.
Maps:	U.S.G.S. 7.5' Quads.: Mount Aire and Park City West. See trail map for "Big Water Trail to Dog Lake" (W-9).
Length/Time:	2.8 mi./45 min. (one way). Allow about 25 min. for return trip.
Elevation Changes:	
High:	8,940' (Park West Overlook)
Low:	7,640' (trailhead)
Change:	1,300'
Overall Difficulty:	Moderate/difficult.
Technical Difficulty:	Moderate/technical.

ALTHOUGH A SHORT TRAIL, just about three miles, there are more than enough challenges for the average or advanced rider, including four major water crossings, steep unrideable hills, and rocky and rough trail conditions. Yet, the appeal of this ride is that it provides access to the Wasatch Crest Trail from the Park West Overlook. From the ridgeline the possibilities are numerous (See Wasatch Crest Trail W-11).

The Wasatch Crest Trail between Mill Creek and Big Cottonwood canyons.

Description

Start at the Upper Mill Creek parking lot. Pass through the rock barriers directly on the east side of the lot then ride east on a pseudo-4WD up the canyon drainage. (Note: This route immediately crosses about a mile of private property before continuing on public Forest Service lands up to the ridgeline. Also, sheepherding is permitted in this upper canyon area.)

Initially, the path is smooth and flat, but after a short distance that changes with the first of four water crossings (all are rocky and deep but rideable, if you don't hesitate). Proceed up the canyon crossing the creek a second and third time (the latter the product of a beaver dam) then yet a fourth time about **1.0** miles from the trailhead (very rocky and technical, walking recommended). Now you face the most difficult section of the trail, a rock strewn wall 300 yards long and seemingly impossible to ride. If you *can* ride this stretch without touching down, you're ready for the NORBA Nationals. Don't feel too humbled by dismounting early and pushing it. Once on top, the trail levels considerably but still contains a few short steep ascents. **1.5** miles from the trailhead the climbing subsides as you break out into a broad clearing marked by a 4WD branching to the right (southeast). This 4WD is the return route of the Upper Mill Creek Basin Trail discussed as Option W-11.2 under the Wasatch Crest Trail. However, continue on the main 4WD heading northeast up the canyon rising gently to the Park West Overlook one mile away (**m 2.8**). Take a break and enjoy the view.

Option W-10.1: Park West Resort: (difficult, moderate/technical).

Descending through the Park West Ski Resort along its many 4WD access roads is a difficult, steep, rocky option. Just remember, when you reach the base of the resort, there are three options: 1) grunt your way back up through the resort to the pass, then down Mill Creek Canyon, 2) ride some twenty to thirty miles of paved road down Parley's Canyon along I-80 and then back up Mill Creek Canyon to the parking area (or, if you planned ahead, have a shuttle set up along the way), or 3) spend the evening in Park City and worry about it tomorrow.

Option W-11: See Wasatch Crest Trail.

Wasatch Crest Trail

Trail Number:	W-11 (The Ridgeline)
Location:	Between Upper Mill Creek Canyon and Big Cottonwood Canyon (Guardsman's Pass).
Access/Parking:	See access for both the Big Water and Upper Mill Creek Trails.
Trailhead:	The ridgeline trail begins at the Park West Overlook at the top of Upper Mill Creek Canyon, about 2.8 miles from the parking area (see Upper Mill Creek Canyon Trail).
Type:	Out and back with optional loops, 4WD and single track.
Land Status:	U.S.F.S. and private property.
Maps:	U.S.G.S. 7.5' Quads.: Brighton and Park City West, Utah, Dromedary Peak and Mount Aire for options. See trail map for "Big Water Trail to Dog Lake" (W-9).
Length/Time:	6.3 mi./1 hr. 30 min. (one way). Allow the same amount of time for the return trip but much more time for one or several options.

Elevation Changes:		
High:	9,920'	(Peak VABM 10006, Silver)
Low:	8,930'	(trailhead)
Change:	990'	(Note: Typical of ridge trails, the total elevation gain, about 2,500', greatly exceeds the net elevation gain.)

Overall Difficulty:	Moderate/difficult.
Technical Difficulty:	Moderate/technical.

THE CREST TRAIL contains equal amounts of 4WD road and narrow, often exposed, single track. Many climbs and descents are very rocky and steep, requiring both advanced riding skills and the tolerance to push your bike. This ride upgrades to difficult when incorporating one or more options. Without question, the best view into the heart of the Central Wasatch Range is from the Wasatch Crest.

Description

The Wasatch Crest Trail begins at the Park West Overlook marked by a small saddle and a large clearing, but getting to the trailhead is no easy task. Expect to push large portions of the Upper Mill Creek Trail (W-10), as it contains many steep technical sections and four challenging water crossings.

From the Park West Overlook the trail heads south into the evergreens up a moderately difficult 4WD. After about 0.5 mile, the road reaches a small saddle offering excellent views of the Park West Ski Resort, the Park City Valley, and the High Uintas to the east. Continuing south along the undulating ridgeline, a 4WD branches east from a second small saddle (m 1.0) and descends to Red Pine Lake (private property), but stay on the ridgeline trail, now a rough single track. This is the first of two decision points, as beyond here the trail becomes considerably more difficult. Immediately south of here you face a short but very steep, very technical, and intimidating hill. Surmounting this hill, the trail levels somewhat, rolling along the ridge. It contains many more technical stretches where imbedded rocks are large and make for often difficult walking, but push on as the best is yet to come. The climbing culminates, temporarily, as you break out onto the ridgeline above and north of Lake Desolation (m 2.3). Now for decision two, continue or turn back.

For hearty souls choosing to continue, drop down the narrow ridgeline single track into the saddle above and northeast of Lake Desolation. In this saddle is exposed the northeasterly dipping beds of white and maroon sandstones and siltstones of the Triassic age Ankerah Formation, and just over the east edge of the ridge an exposed face of sandstone shows perfectly preserved ripple marks—indicative of an ancient, shallow marine depositional environment. Also, note a trail branching to the northwest from this saddle. This single track drops through the aspens and down to Lake Desolation and is discussed as Option W-11.1. Onward.

Rising out of the saddle, above Lake Desolation, to the south and back up onto the ridgeline is perhaps the most difficult and technical section of the ride. Play it safe and commit to walking before you are forced off, or thrown from, your bike as the jagged, barren sandstone creates potentially dangerous conditions. Just remember, you chose to continue, and the pay-off is soon to come.

One of the premier single tracks the Wasatch has to offer.

Leaving Lake Desolation behind, the Wasatch Crest Trail rounds Peak 9990 where you are treated to the first view of the dynamic and jagged Cottonwood Ridgeline to the south. The urge to burst out into song like Julie Andrews in *The Sound of Music* is overwhelming.

The next three miles are the highlight of the ride and offer by far the most spectacular view into the heart of the Central Wasatch Range. Although elevation changes are slight, the narrow, exposed single track hugs the sharp ridgeline, contours around lesser peaks, and passes through open slopes laden with vibrant wildflowers in the spring and stands of dense aspens shimmering golden in the fall. Only a skillful rider can negotiate this moderate/technical trail while letting one eye wander to catch sporadic glimpses of the rugged Cottonwood Ridgeline to the south and the cuspate basins of Mt. Raymond and Gobblers Knob to the west. Above West Monitor Flat (a glacially scoured valley), the single track grades back to a 4WD, then rounds the radio facilities and Scott's Hill denoting the end of the trail (**m 6.3**). The 4WD continues south, dropping into Scott's Pass and then southwest, exiting onto the paved Gaurdsman's Pass Road at the second right hand switchback two miles up from Big Cottonwood Road (**m 7.6**). Be forewarned that continuing this route crosses private property (posted) and several mining claims.

Option W-11.1: Lake Desolation/Mill D (single track, 4.1 mi./45 min. one way, (-)2,330', moderate/difficult, moderate/technical). See Option W-9.2 as described in the Big Water Trail, also.

Although marked on topographic maps, the Lake Desolation Trail descending from the Wasatch Crest has since been abandoned. The existing trail begins in the saddle northeast of Lake Desolation and forks from the Crest Trail to the northwest. As the single track turns south downhill, it becomes very steep with much loose dirt, sand, and rocks. To prevent unnecessary erosion, and for your own safety, walk the majority of this descent. Once in the aspens the path switches back a few times and is more rideable as it drops to the northwest side of Lake Desolation.

Follow the Lake Desolation Trail west for about 1.0 mile across open meadows, in and out of fir and aspens, and down several short, steep, often rocky hills to the Lake Desolation/Big Cottonwood Road (Mill D) junction. Log water bars are numerous and typically at an angle to the trail, thus ride cautiously and attack them at right angles to prevent your wheels from sliding out from under you. Never ride around water bars as this accelerates the erosion they are trying to control.

Descending Mill D to Big Cottonwood Canyon is easy at first, but becomes progressively more difficult and technical. After 0.5 mile, the path

Above Lake Desolation along the Wasatch Crest Trail.

veers uphill on the west side of the drainage, hugs the exposed slope, and becomes very narrow in spots. As the trail wraps around to the west, it descends sharply, crosses numerous exposed roots and log water bars, then exits Reynold's Gulch at the "Meeting of the Glaciers" sign.

As opting to return up Mill D past Lake Desolation and up onto the ridgeline again is a *gonzo*-plus attempt, have a shuttle set up or consider returning to the Wasatch Crest via Big Cottonwood Road and Guardsman's Pass. When started from the Big Cottonwood Canyon side on Guardsman's Road, the sixteen mile Wasatch Crest to Mill D loop is one of the finest in the Wasatch. But be aware of private property limitations adjacent to Guardsman's Road.

Option W-11.2:   Upper Mill Creek Basin (4WD, single track, 1.4 mi./20 min., (-)1120', moderate, moderate).

From atop the ridgeline directly north of Lake Desolation (**m 2.3**), a faded single track branches west just before the pines, then immediately turns south heading back to Lake Desolation. Instead, turn north following a vague single track, paralleling the ridgeline trail but just to the west of it, into the pines and across a few fallen trees. This obscure trail soon turns west and descends along a lesser ridge toward Peak 9467 as labeled on topographic maps. In a small saddle on this east-west trending ridge, the path switches back sharply to the east then descends steeply into the upper Mill Creek Basin.

(Note: The first mile of this option is a moderate/technical single track, but once down in the basin the path follows a less difficult but rustic 4WD northwest and connects with the Upper Mill Creek Trail about 1.5 miles above the parking area.)

Option W-11.3: The Ultimate Loop (loop, paved, 4WD, single track, 23 mi./3 hrs. 30 min., difficult, moderate/technical).

By far the best loop in the Wasatch is a combination of the Wasatch Crest, Upper Mill Creek, and Big Water Trails.

If accessing the Wasatch Crest Trail from the Big Cottonwood side, begin just north of Scott's Hill, follow the ridgeline north past Lake Desolation to the Park West Overlook, then descend west through Upper Mill Creek Canyon to the paved parking area. Ride the Big Water Trail past Dog Lake and down to the Lake Desolation/Mill D junction. Descend Mill D Canyon exiting through Reynold's Gulch, and culminate the trip on the smooth, paved Big Cottonwood Canyon Road. A strategic parking location is Solitude Ski Resort, splitting the amount of paved riding up to Guardsman's Road, thus concluding the ride with the option of stopping into "The Bar" at Solitude to refresh your body and soul and reminisce the day's adventure.

(Note: The Wasatch Crest, Lake Desolation and Mill D trails are very popular multi-use trails. On weekends the congestion is often overwhelming. Please use caution, be courteous to other trail users, ride in control, and at all times ride in a manner to minimize trail erosion.)

(Final Note: Many feel that accessing the Wasatch Crest from the Big Cottonwood side via Guardsman's Road and Scott's Pass is preferable to accessing it from Upper Mill Creek Canyon, but be aware of the land status restrictions around this area.)

Brighton to Solitude

Trail Number:	W-12
Location/Access:	Travel 15 miles to the top of Big Cottonwood Canyon Road (S.R. 190, 7200 South and about 3700 East) to the Brighton Village Store & Cafe.
Parking:	At or near the store.
Trailhead:	The ride begins across the road (northwest) from the store, past a chain link gate posted "No Parking," on a paved drive accessing the summer homes area.
Type:	Loop, single track, 4WD and paved.
Land Status:	U.S.F.S., Solitude Ski Resort, and private property.
Maps:	U.S.G.S. 7.5' Quads.: Brighton and Park City West, Utah.
Length/Time:	5.3 mi./1 hr.
Elevation Changes:	
High:	9,000' (under the Sunrise lift at Solitude)
Low:	8,080' (base of Inspiration lift at Solitude)
Change:	920'
Trailhead:	8,730'
Overall Difficulty:	Moderate.
Technical Difficulty:	Moderate/technical.

DON'T LET THE MODERATE/TECHNICAL RATING scare you. The single track from Silver Lake to Solitude is full of large imbedded rocks, a challenge to navigate, creating an observed trials-like course. Dropping through Solitude is along typical loose, rocky, 4WD resort access roads. Few settings compare to that of Silver Lake near the trail's beginning.

Description

For being such a short trail, it is perhaps the hardest to describe.

Cross the chain link gate, head north on the narrow paved drive for a few hundred yards, then turn left (west) on a wide flat dirt path immediately after crossing over a small creek. Ride around the north side of Silver Lake to where the trail splits (**m 0.2**). The left fork circumnavigates Silver Lake (Option W-12.1); the right fork (main route) heads north over a rocky stretch, switches back south after a few hundred feet, then immediately turns right (west) heading into thick aspens. Confused? Note: If you exit onto a road accessing summer homes, you've gone too far north; if you begin climbing above the west shore of Silver Lake, you've gone too far south.

Heading northwest toward Solitude, the single track rises gently but is technical due to many large embedded rocks and exposed roots. Although dismounting—as your wheels get hung up—is frustrating, back up and attack each little challenge several times until you find the proper line and proper gears. Important: Know the clearance of your chain rings through here.

About 0.8 mile from the trailhead, the path splits near a pile of sawed up tree trunks and a sign posted "Warning closed area, no avalanche control". The right fork (Sol-Bright Trail) soon fades out into thick brush requiring much cross-country bushwhacking, not a good idea. The left (main) trail continues to rise through the aspens, is less technical, and an enjoyable smooth single track.

Ride under the Sunrise chair lift and past a very small white sign directing you to Lake Solitude. At the Deer Run (**m 1.0**) ski trail marker, the path becomes extremely rocky, technical, and rises steeply to Lake Solitude. This route means pushing—lots of pushing. Instead, exit to the right (west) directly to the base of the Summit chair lift. Lake Solitude lies a few hundred yards up the access road—a steep, difficult climb.

Now, from the base of the Summit lift, ride northwest down through the trees contouring the face of the mountain, cross under the Powderhorn lift and out onto the Main Street ski run. As Main Street heads downhill, turn left (west, **m 2.1**) on the Wanderer Cut-off, pass under the Moonbeam chair, and wave hello to Big Bird on Sesame Street.

Past Big Bird, fork right, pass under the Inspiration chair, and descend across the runs Rumble and Grumble (good names because the 4WD dropping to the base of the Inspiration lift, **m 2.9**, steepens and becomes quite rocky). At the bottom, ride about 0.5 mile east to the resort's main base facilities (**m 3.6**). From Solitude, the Brighton Village Store is 1.7 miles up Big Cottonwood Road.

[Note: What makes this ride most appealing is not one but two places to stop and relax: the base facilities at Solitude ("The Bar"—an original name) and the Brighton Village Store & Cafe. Both offer plenty of cold drinks, hot food, munchies galore, and friendly atmospheres.]

Option W-12.1:   Silver Lake Trail (out and back, single track, 0.5 mi./5 min. one way, easy, minor/moderate).

On the north side of Silver Lake, a single track branches left (about **0.2** mile from the paved summer homes road) and contours the west side of the lake. It's a short ride, but a mini observed trials-like course with numerous exposed roots and very short climbs which really require you to know how to handle your bike. On the south side of the lake the path crosses an opening among the pines and onto a paved drive clearly marked "Private, No trespassing, No camping." Avoid any conflict by returning on the same path back around the lake thus staying on U.S.F.S. land.

Placid, Silver Lake.

Option W-12.2: Silver Fork Canyon (out and back, 4WD, 2.1 mi./20 min. one way, 350', easy, minor).

From the lower Solitude parking lot, follow a dirt road around the base of the Inspiration chair lift (described as m **2.9**, previously) then onto a narrow paved drive accessing summer homes (private property). The road turns back to dirt (4WD) as it heads south, up Silver Fork Canyon, passing through thick conifers and pastel wildflowers (cow parsnip, sticky geranium, and sunflower). The road ends at a mine adit (barred and locked). Return the same way. [Note: About half way up the canyon road a trail accessing Honeycomb Canyon branches to the left (southeast) and crosses the stream. This option is a very difficult bike ride, but an enjoyable hike, as the trail soon passes under the precipitous Honeycomb Cliffs.]

Option W-12.3: Solitude's Summit Lift Road (for the real *gonzos*).

Instead of heading to the base of Solitude from the Summit chair lift near Lake Solitude, ride up to the top of the lift along the steep, switchbacking, 4WD access road (difficult, very loose dirt and rocks). Once at the top, options include following a vague single track southwest then down Grizzly Gulch to Alta (difficult and technical), or heading east along the upper Sol-Bright Trail descending to Twin Lakes then down to Brighton (moderately difficult, but again very loose trail material).

Option W-12.4: Brighton Ski Resort.

Like other resorts, Brighton hosts a number of dirt access roads crisscrossing its ski runs; most are loose dirt, steep and difficult. An enticing ride is the nature trail leading from the base of Brighton to Lake Mary then up to Lake Catherine. Although one of the most popular and beautiful day hikes in the central Wasatch, the Forest Service does not recommend this route as a mountain bike trail. Approaching Lake Mary is steep, very rocky, and requires you to shoulder your bike for some distance. The same is true when trying to surmount Catherine's Pass en route to Alta. Remember, there are many other trails more suited to mountain bikes than this fragile location.

BRIGHTON VILLAGE STORE & CAFE
Bike rentals and service ▪ Hot lunches and supplies
Brighton, Utah 84121 ▪ (801) 649-9156
Observe all trail use and land status signs

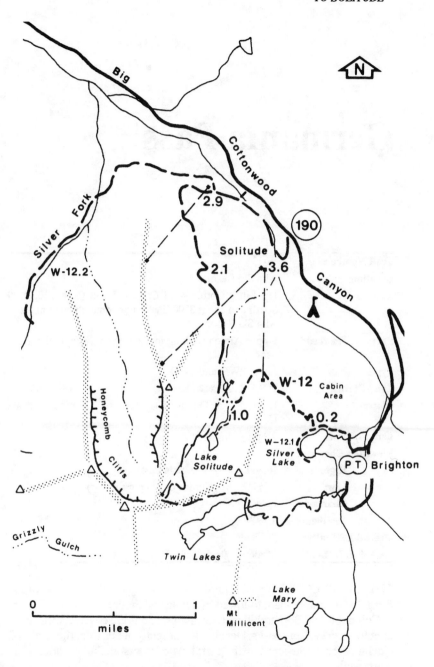

Brighton—Solitude Ski Resort

Germania Pass

Trail Number:	W-13
Location:	Alta Ski Resort.
Access:	Up Little Cottonwood Canyon Road (S.R. 210, 9200 South and about 3700 East) approximately nine miles to Alta Ski Resort.
Parking/Trailhead:	Upper Albion parking lot near the Grizzly Gulch trailhead.
Type:	Loop, 2WD and 4WD.
Land Status:	U.S.F.S., Alta Ski Resort.
Maps:	U.S.G.S. 7.5' Quads.: Brighton and Dromedary Peak, Utah.
Length/Time:	9.0 mi./1 hr. 45 min.
Elevation Changes:	

High:	10,380'	(Germania Pass)
Low:	8,550'	(Collins Gulch parking lot)
Change:	1,830'	
Trailhead:	8,760'	

Overall Difficulty:	Difficult.
Technical Difficulty:	Moderate/technical.

THE LOOP CONSISTS of a moderate to steep climb through Albion Basin to Germania Pass, followed by a long and moderately steep descent of Collins Gulch. Both uphill and downhill sections are covered with abundant loose gravel and rocks. Despite the difficulty of this ride, the textbook glacial terrain carpeted with pastel wildflowers make it more than worthwhile.

Devils Castle stands watch over Secret Lake.

Description

From the parking area near Grizzly Gulch, the ride follows a graded 2WD providing access to the Albion Basin U.S.F.S. campground. This section is very easy with virtually no technical difficulty, only occasional washboard.

At **m 2.2**, just past the summit of the Sunnyside chair lift, follow a 4WD that branches to the right (west) past a red iron gate and to the base of the Sugarloaf chair lift (**m 2.7**). Here, the 4WD access road heads south and west, switchbacks up through Greeley Bowl past a few mine workings, then passes up and under the Sugarloaf chair lift (**m 4.1**). The last two miles are steep, difficult, and often very rocky.

Under the Sugarloaf chair lift, stop, take a break, and soak up the 360 degree panoramic view of Albion Basin—classic alpine glacial terrain. The semi-circular bowl, shaped basin is a cirque which represents the accumulation area of a glacial trough that once extended down and scoured out the U-shaped Little Cottonwood Canyon. The basin is bound by the steep headwalls of Supreme Ridge, Devils Castle, and Greeley Ridge. Left behind in this depression is Secret Lake, a glacial lake or tarn. Notice that many of the rock outcroppings in this area are smooth and contain long parallel scratches and small chip marks. These indicate scouring and scratching from rocks dragged along the base of the once overlying glacier.

The trail proceeds steeply up and under the lift, then levels as it crests Germania Pass to the west (**m 5.1**).

From Germania Pass the Collins Gulch 4WD trail descends several very rocky switchbacks, contours through Ballroom Bowl, then descends under the Germania chair lift. At two switchbacks under the lift, the trail splits (always follow the main road branching left). Halfway down, the trail passes the base of the Germania lift (**m 6.8**). Let your hands and back rest from the pounding descent while basking in the sun and sipping a cool beverage of your choice at the Watson Shelter, open during the summer months serving drinks and snacks. Check for hours of operation.

Continuing down, the road is less steep but still very rocky as it winds down the valley then crosses the base of the ominous ski run "Alf's High Rustler." Exit onto the Collins parking lot (**m 8.0**), turn right (east) past Gold Miner's Daughter Lodge, and follow the dirt road paralleling the rope tow back to the upper Albion parking area.

[Note: As with any loop, this trail may be ridden in either direction. Ascending Collins Gulch (riding the trail in reverse) is by far much steeper and more difficult.]

**Action during the two-day Alta-Rustler Run
mountain bike race.**

Option W-13.1:   Albion Basin (loop, 2WD and 4WD, 4.8 mi./45 min., easy, minor/moderate).

The Germania Pass trail is for the experienced rider, obviously.

Instead of turning right on the 4WD road accessing the base of the Sugarloaf chair (**m 2.2**), continue straight and into the U.S.F.S. campground. The campground road is an easy 0.6 mile loop passing through tall Subalpine fir and about two dozen designated campsites. Although many spur roads exist, most of these lead to summer homes and should be respected as private property. Instead, take the trail leading up to Secret Lake. Most of this trail is difficult, technical, and not rideable. Lock your bike to a sturdy tree and hike the short trail to the glacial lake.

When returning to the parking area from the campground loop, *now* take the turnoff for the Sugarloaf chair, but fork right just before dropping to the chair lift's base along a 4WD paralleling Little Cottonwood drainage to the northwest. This descent (moderately technical—some loose rocks) exits at a red gate onto the 2WD access road at its first switchback, **0.4** mile above the parking area.

Option W-13.2:   Catherine's Pass.

This is a very difficult ride that begins east of the entrance to the Albion Basin campground, heads east over Catherine's Pass, and eventually drops to the Brighton Ski Resort at the top of Big Cottonwood Canyon (a *gonzo* ride for those who don't mind pushing and carrying their bike). However, the Forest Service does not encourage nor recommend this trail due to its severity and potential for erosion. This is a better hiking than biking route.

[Note: Both the Germania Pass (ridden in reverse) and the Albion Basin loop (minus the campground loop) rides are portions of the two day, NORBA sanctioned, Alta-Rustler Run mountain bike race held annually.]

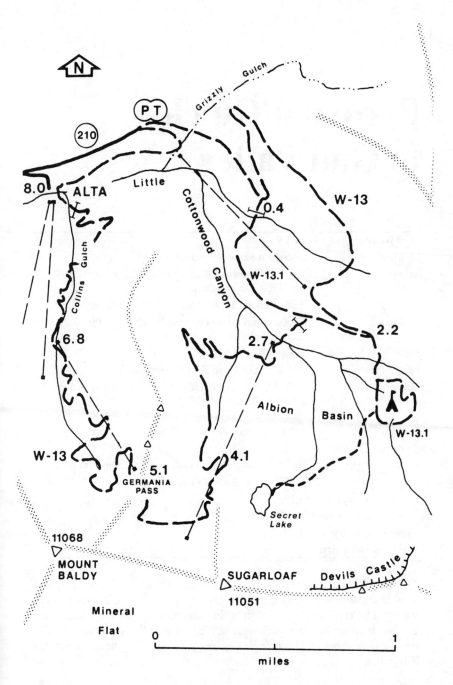

Alta Ski Resort

Peruvian Gulch to Gad Valley

Trail Number:	W-14
Location:	Snowbird Ski and Summer Resort.
Access:	Little Cottonwood Canyon (S.R. 210, about 9200 South and 3700 East) to Snowbird.
Parking:	Main parking area for Snowbird Plaza (Entry Level 2).
Trailhead:	Dirt access road for Peruvian Gulch above the Black Jack Condominiums.
Type:	Loop, 4WD and paved (minor).
Land Status:	U.S.F.S., Snowbird Ski and Summer Resort.
Maps:	U.S.G.S. 7.5' Quad.: Dromedary Peak, Utah. Additional resort trail maps available at the Activity Center on the Plaza.
Length/Time:	4.2 mi./50 min. Allow much more time for options.
Elevation Changes:	
High:	9,000' (Peruvian Gulch at Rothman Way)
Low:	7,850' (Base of Gad chair lifts)
Change:	1,150'
Trailhead:	8,600'
Overall Difficulty:	Difficult.
Technical Difficulty:	Moderate.

ALTHOUGH PERUVIAN GULCH is steeper than Gad Valley, it is shorter and allows for a longer and more enjoyable downhill through Gad Valley. The trails at Snowbird pass through deeply scoured, rugged glacial bowls covered with wildflowers in the spring and provide an uninterrupted panorama of the complex geology comprising the Cottonwood Ridgeline.

Descending Dick Bass Highway to the Plaza at Snowbird, backdropped by the Hellgate Cliffs.

Description

(Note: There are no easy mountain bike routes at Snowbird. All trails should be classified "a serious workout.")

Cross the bridge at the east end of the parking lot, ride the dirt access road past the Tram and Cliff Lodge, and pedal up the paved Alta Bypass road past the Black Jack Condos to the right (south). A 4WD access road begins at a chain gate and proceeds up the east side of Peruvian Gulch.

The ascent is difficult; the grade is consistently steep without any notable breaks, plus the loose gravel offers poor traction. Expect to push portions unless you're in top physical condition. 0.7 mile up Peruvian Gulch the road levels, intersects Rothman Way ski trail heading west, or switches back northeast accessing the Tram summit on Hidden Peak (Option W-14.1).

Initially, descending Rothman Way is steep and very rocky. Shortly, the path levels to an easy cruise down to the Wilbere Chair Lift summit (**m 1.4**). The 4WD branching uphill to the southeast accesses the Mid-Gad Restaurant and a trail leading into Upper Gad Valley (Option W-14.2).

Travel 0.2 mile downhill to the southeast along Dick Bass Highway to the open ski slope Big Emma. The single track heading north is the continuation of Dick Bass Highway—an optional descent to the plaza, the last 300 feet of which is steep, rocky, and technical. Crossing Big Emma, the 4WD access road passes under the Gad lifts then descends Gad Valley through a series of four moderately difficult switchbacks. Once at the base (**m 2.7**), follow the paved road east through the parking lots back to the plaza.

Option W-14.1:   The Tram to Hidden Peak (this is truly a *gonzo* ride, out and back, 4WD, 2.9 mi./1 hr. 20 min. one way, +2,000', very difficult, moderate).

Call it what you want (and when you reach the top, what you call it probably should not be said in public), ascending the tram is tough and for the serious biker only. From the plaza to the summit of Hidden Peak is a gain of 2,900' in 4.5 miles, a 12.0 percent grade on the average.

Where the Peruvian access road joins with Rothman Way (**m 0.7**), turn left following the 4WD as it switches back north then immediately south. The next mile or so is a good sampling of what lies ahead (a consistently steep, dirt/gravel 4WD road, or in simpler terms—a long grunt).

About 0.5 mile above the switchbacks on the right side of the trail, dark gray/brown outcrops of Cambrian Ophir shale show wavy laminations of siltstone (ripple marks?), whereas on the left side of the trail Cambrian Maxfield Limestone comprises the gray/green bedded cliffs. Typically, all the rock layers are tilted to the east/northeast.

**Choose either the easy or hard way to the top of
Hidden Peak at Snowbird.**

The trail flattens temporarily crossing Chip's Run and Primrose Path, then resumes its very steep climb on the east side of the Cirque Basin. Although quite intimidating, the switchbacks ascending the upper Cirque are easier than they appear, but still difficult overall. Once atop the Cirque, under the last Tram tower, the final several hundred yards require walking—just too steep and extremely rocky (m 2.9).

Of course, the 360 degree panoramic view from the Tram summit is outstanding. Mineral Basin drops down into American Fork Canyon to the south, while Mt. Baldy and Sugarloaf mark the Alta Ski Resort boundary to the east. To the north, the Cottonwood Ridgeline is composed of tilted brown and tan sedimentary beds of the Big Cottonwood Formation comprising Superior Peak with light gray quartz-monzonite of the Little Cottonwood stock below and west of Superior. Behind the Cliff Lodge, white and gray banded Mississippian limestones of the Hell Gate Cliffs are overlain by brown Mineral Fork tillite. If this sounds confusing, it is; but this complex geology, where numerous faults juxtapose rock units of many different periods, is what makes the Wasatch Mountains so attractive and distinct.

While on top of Hidden Peak, don't be surprised if you receive quizzical glares from tourists stepping off the Tram, because the last thing they expect to see up here is a mountain bike. A typical exchange of words might be:

"Now, I thought bikes were not allowed on the tram," says the tourist.

"That's right, they're not," you reply.

"Then how'd you get . . . no, you didn't really ride . . . ."

"Yup. Don't ask me why, but it seemed like a good thing to do at the time!"

Then, hop on your bike and whisk away while their jaws flap in the breeze, or really ham it up and pose for a few photos or home movies.

(Note: Once on top of Hidden Peak, tram rides down are free and bicycles are allowed. Yet, bikes are not allowed on the tram at the Plaza for the ride up to its summit.)

Option W-14.2:   Upper Gad Valley (out and back, 4WD, 2.5 mi./1 hr. one way, 1,320', difficult, moderate/technical)

At the top of the Wilbere chair (m 1.4), turn south pedaling uphill. The first 0.3 mile is steep and difficult but technically minor. Then heading west across Big Emma ski run, the road flattens considerably. As it turns south approaching the Mid-Gad Restaurant (m 0.5), a 4WD branches to the right (west) descending to the Gad II chair access road. Turn left (southwest) in the bottom of this hollow to begin the ascent to the Gad II chair summit. This climb is steep with abundant loose rocks, switches back and forth above Gad Valley Gulch, crosses Gadzooks ski run, then climbs to the top of the chair lift (**m 2.5**). As difficult as the ride is, the glacial setting, tall Subalpine fir, and colorful wildflowers dotting the alpine meadow magnify the serenity of Snowbird. Geologically, Gad Valley sits entirely within the gray quartz-monzonite of the Little Cottonwood Stock.

If you're *gonzo* enough to tackle the entire mountain with all of its options in one day, no doubt you'll be a tad bit hungry and dry. Even though Snowbird boasts to be a great winter ski resort, most of its restaurants and shops are open during the warm season as well. The Plaza seems to be the most popular and casual gathering place and is where most of the summer's activities are held. Don't miss out on Snowbird's annual Octoberfest celebration complete with dancing, beer chugging, bratwurst and sauerkraut, and of course revelling oom-pah bands.

(Note: Mountain bike rentals are available at the Activities Center located on the east side of the Plaza.)

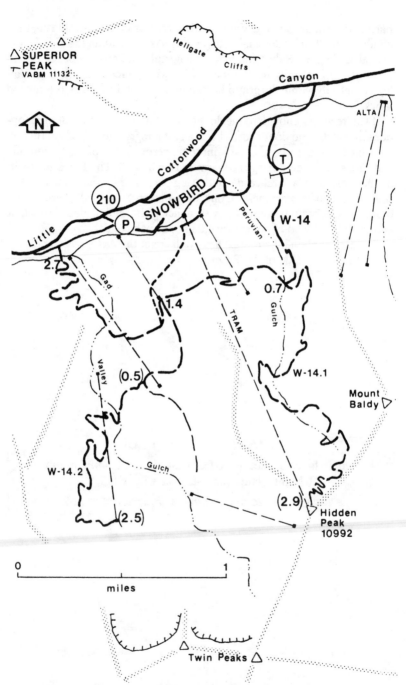

Snowbird Ski and Summer Resort

Upper Corner Canyon Road

Trail Number:	W-15
Location:	East of Draper City then along the base of Lone Peak and over the Traverse Mountains to the town of Alpine.
Access:	South on I-15, exit for 106th South Street. Head east on 106th South Street, right (south) on 1700 East, left (east) on Pioneer Avenue (12300 South in Draper), then 0.7 mile to the end of paved road.
Parking/Trailhead:	At the end of Pioneer Avenue, a small dirt turnaround on the south (right) side of the road, near a yellow public notice sign, marks the trailhead. Park at your own discretion due to private property limitations.
Type:	Out and back, 4WD.
Land Status:	City of Draper, public access road. Note: All land adjacent to this road is private property.
Map:	U.S.G.S. 7.5' Quads.: Draper and Lehi, Utah.
Length/Time:	7.3 mi./1 hr. 10 min. (one way, Draper to Alpine). Allow the same amount of time for the return trip.
Elevation Changes:	
High:	5,855' (Corner Canyon/Hog Hollow Pass)
Low:	4,700' (trailhead)
Change:	1,155'
Overall Difficulty:	Easy/moderate.
Technical Difficulty:	Minor/moderate.

THE MAIN ROUTE follows the dirt/gravel 4WD Upper Corner Canyon Road—a long consistent grade with a few rocky and rutted sections. From Alpine, ascending Hog Hollow Road to the Pass is shorter and easier than from Draper.

Description

Begin by heading southeast on a 4WD past a yellow public notice sign through scrub oak. Once through the brush, the Upper Corner Canyon Road is obvious and heads south. 0.3 mile from the trailhead a 4WD branches right, crosses private property, accesses the old Corner Canyon Road below, and is notorious for thick, frustrating sand traps. **0.6** mile from the trailhead a second dirt road forks right (southwest) and is the access/maintenance road paralleling the Salt Lake City Metropolitan Water District aqueduct, a return trail discussed as Option W-15.1.

Continue up Corner Canyon Road as it wraps around the southwest flank of Lone Peak. The ascent is consistent but only minor to moderately difficult and minor to moderately technical due to a few sand traps and some exposed bedrock in the road. At **m 3.3** the road crosses Corner Canyon Creek, marked by a drainage pipe extending from the hillside, then becomes severely rutted approaching the Corner Canyon/Hog Hollow Pass (obviously, a few vehicles have had a difficult time through here on a wet, rainy day making the road a roller coaster of a bike ride).

[Note: 0.2 mile before the Pass, two parallel 4WD trails branch to the north and downhill. The lower (more easterly) trail begins an optional return route following a gas pipeline down into Corner Canyon.]

The Corner Canyon/Hog Hollow Pass (**m 4.1**) is marked by a large flat clearing and a four-way intersection of dirt roads. This area has been used extensively by ORV's judging from the numerous trails crisscrossing the hillsides, but remember all land through here is privately owned. Hog Hollow Road continues straight (south), immediately bends to the southeast, then descends 3.2 miles to the town of Alpine (**m 7.3**). Essentially a smooth, gradual 2WD its entire length, Hog Hollow is popular with ORV's, so be careful rounding blind corners, keep your eyes and ears open, and make your presence known to other travelers.

Once in Alpine, Hog Hollow Road is the only way back to Draper for all practical purposes.

Option W-15.1: Pipeline/aqueduct maintenance roads (private property, 4WD, 3.0 mi./30 min. one way, moderate/difficult, moderate/technical).

Following the gas pipeline and aqueduct maintenance roads, this return route is much more challenging than back tracking down the Upper Corner Canyon Road.

Approximately 0.2 mile northeast of the Corner Canyon/Hog Hollow Pass, two trails branch downhill and to the north from the Upper Corner Canyon Road. The lower or more easterly trail is the preferred descent.

The western face of Mt. Timpanogos as viewed from the Traverse Mountains.

Still, this 4WD descends steeply, is very rocky for the most part, then grades to a very narrow, technical single track as it drops into an eroded, overgrown gully. After one mile the pipeline road exits next to Corner Canyon Creek (flowing) at a posted wooden fenceline closing the upper drainage for vegetation and erosion control. Although crossing the creek is tempting here, ride the trail downhill (west) for about 0.2 mile to a second posted wooden fence. Now, cross the creek and parallel it a short distance at which point you face a very steep, intimidating hill.

You guessed it, push your way up the hill (too sandy and too steep to ride). Once on top, follow the sandy, 4WD maintenance road north gradually descending in elevation for about 1.5 miles to the junction with Corner Canyon Road 0.6 mile above the parking area.

Even though intuition suggests following the old Corner Canyon Road below (instead of crossing the creek and pushing up the hill along the aqueduct maintenance road), the aqueduct road is actually an easier return route as the old road contains many thick sand traps that bog down even the knobbiest of tires.

Option W-15.2: Traverse Mountains Ridge Road (private property, out and back, 4WD, 3.5 mi./45 min. one way, 830', moderate/difficult, moderate/technical).

From the Corner Canyon/Hog Hollow Pass, a 4WD heads west up onto the ridge. Although many trails branch to either side, the main road is the more obvious, well worn path. After about two miles along the undulating ridge, the road turns south then west again, and begins a steep, rocky, technical climb for an additional mile, ending in a small grassy clearing (about 3.0 miles from the Pass). This option culminates with a short but very steep climb onto the peak directly to the south capped with a red pyramid bench mark (Peak VABM 6682).

But what is the point of this grunt? Once on top, the uninterrupted 360 degree panoramic view of both the Salt Lake and Provo Valleys plus full views of both the Oquirrh and Wasatch Ranges is staggering, perhaps the most scenic vantage point along the Wasatch Front.

When Brigham Young and the Mormon Pioneers descended Emigration Canyon they obviously had not explored the Traverse Mountains as "This *really* is the place!"

A picture is worth a thousand words, but even a picture does not do justice to this tremendous vista. The Salt Lake and Provo Valleys stretch out to the north and south, respectively, while the vertical granite columns of Lone Peak loom to the east. Mt. Timpanogos with its characteristic horizontal limestone layering dominates the southeast; whereas, Mt. Nebo, the tallest of the Wasatch peaks, caps the southern skyline.

Extending the trip even further (make sure you have plenty of water), wrap around the southwestern flank of Peak VABM 6682 and descend Dry Hollow to the south, exiting onto a 4WD heading east just above and bordering the sprawling farm fields. This moderate/difficult 4WD eventually connects with Hog Hollow Road just above Alpine and is a confusing route even with a map.

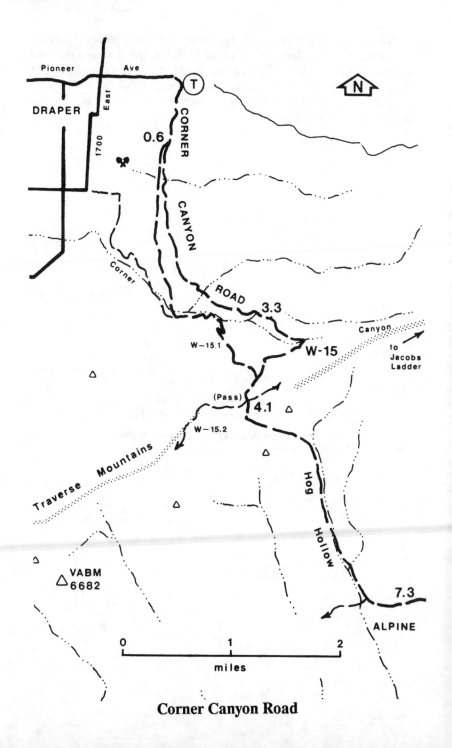

Corner Canyon Road

Mill Canyon Peak

Trail Number:	W-16 (Upper American Fork Canyon Ridgeline)
Location:	North Fork of American Fork Canyon.
Access:	I-15 south, exit #287 for Alpine/Highland, east on S.R. 92 into American Fork Canyon. Five miles past the Uinta National Forest sign, turn left on S.R. 144 (North Fork) then travel 2.6 miles to Tibble Fork Reservoir.
Parking:	Provided at Tibble Fork Reservoir, or park at Dutchman's Flat about 4.5 miles from the end of the pavement, thus splitting the elevation gain of American Fork Canyon. A shuttle between these two points is advantageous.
Trailhead:	Dutchman's Flat.
Type:	Loop, 2WD, and single track.
Land Status:	U.S.F.S.
Maps:	U.S.G.S. 7.5' Quads.: Brighton and Aspen Grove, Utah.
Length/Time:	17.5 mi./3 hr. 30 min.
Elevation Changes:	
High:	9,600' (near Mill Canyon Peak)
Low:	6,400' (Tibble Fork Reservoir)
Change:	3,200'
Trailhead:	7,560'
Overall Difficulty:	Difficult.
Technical Difficulty:	Technical.

ALTHOUGH A 2WD DIRT ROAD, American Fork Canyon is steep in spots and generally quite rocky—the easiest portion of this loop. The ridgeline single track is often exposed, narrow, and rocky with many steep sections requiring walking. This portion of the loop is popular with equestrians, so be prepared to dismount and move off the trail in the event of an encounter. Mill Canyon contains numerous log water bars, many of which are up to a foot high, along with abundant exposed roots and rocks. This is one of the most challenging rides among the Wasatch.

Description

Dutchman Flat is a popular area for campers, R.V.s, and equestrians, and provides access into Upper American Fork Canyon, Mary Ellen Gulch, and Mineral Basin and is where this description begins.

American Fork Canyon Road soon crosses the river and splits after 0.5 mile: the left fork continues into Mineral Basin, the right fork (main route) is signed for Baker's Fork. Baker's Fork begins with a series of moderate/difficult switchbacks then climbs steadily for three miles to Pole Line Pass (**m 3.8**). Technical difficulty is minimal.

At Pole Line Pass, the 2WD Baker's Fork road continues northeast (now as Snake Creek Road) descending into Wasatch Mountain State Park; however, the single track portion heads south into scrub oak and aspen following a U.S.F.S. trail sign marked Ridge Trail No. 157. Over the next 0.5 mile, the trail ascends and descends a small but steep hill and is very rocky near Sandy Baker Pass (**m 4.3**). Expect to walk some portions.

At Sandy Baker Pass, a trail marked Pot Hollow forks to the left (southeast). The Ridge Trail, however, forks right (southwest) passing into the pines, then forks again immediately (stay on the left or uphill path). For the next mile, the narrow, exposed single track undulates along the hillside through aspen and fir trees, a fairly easy and most enjoyable stretch. Rounding a small ridge (**m 5.1**), the path drops slightly but stays well above Forest Lake.

Behind and to the northwest, the Alpine Ridge is marked by the Snowbird Tram summit on Hidden Peak. Devils Castle is to the right (east), and American Fork Twin Peaks and Red Baldy are to the left (west). Box Elder Peak rises to over 11,000 feet due west. Cuspate cirques and hanging valleys are evidence of the alpine glaciers that carved and dissected this terrain.

The trail contours the hillside for one mile to the junction (signed) for Forest Lake Trail (**m 6.1, Option W-16.1**). Below, in this basin, a large swath of aspens has been flattened by avalanches and conjures up the eerie feeling when hiking through the tree blast down zone of Mount St.

High above Forest Lake, the Alpine Ridge backdrops one of the Wasatch's most challenging single tracks.

Helens. Do we underestimate the forces of nature?

From the Forest Lake Trail junction the path continues south and becomes very difficult as it crosses a talus field then climbs steeply over a ridge extending northwest from Mill Canyon Peak (**m 6.6**). Surmounting this ridge, a composite view of Mt. Timpanogos (with its deeply scoured glacial valleys), Sundance Ski Resort, and Provo Peak far to the south domineers over the dwindling Alpine Ridgeline to the north.

Rounding the southwest flank of Mill Canyon Peak, the single track remains essentially flat. But it is technical as large boulders create a challenging observed trials-like course. Several faded trails branch from the ridge trail, so stay on what appears to be the main, beaten path.

Past trail junctions for Holman and East Ridge Trail, the Ridge Trail (No. 157) descends the southwest flank of Mill Canyon Peak toward Mill Canyon Spring (**m 9.4**). It is steep at times with sections of abundant loose rocks, and it is safer to walk than bike some sections. As the descent flattens, it winds into Mill Canyon Springs—an open meadow marked by several dirt roads: to the southeast a 4WD drops toward the Cascade Springs Road, to the south a 4WD continues along the Lower American Fork Canyon Ridge Line (Mud Springs Trail, W-17), and to the west a 4WD descends Mill Canyon (the final descent of this loop).

Heading west on Mill Canyon Trail (No. 40), the 4WD turns sharply to the left, changes to a single track, then passes through a meadow following a white diamond trail marker.

Descending Upper Mill Canyon is steep and technical with dozens of log water bars, rocks, and roots to negotiate. Drop your seat down, make sure your helmet and eyeglasses are securely fastened, and swing your weight over the rear tire to prepare for the challenge. About half way down the canyon the trail cuts through another meadow marked by the Holman Trail joining from the north (**m 11.0**).

Lower Mill Canyon is less technical with many flat, smooth sections, a few water crossings, and thickly vegetated hillsides. Finally, the ride down exits onto the rocky, braided stream bed of American Fork Canyon River above Tibble Fork Reservoir (**m 13.0**). Picking a dry path across the river bottom may be difficult to impossible in spring and early summer.

The loop is completed by grinding 4.5 miles up American Fork Canyon, a long, tiring, bumpy ride. Now you know why a car shuttle is advantageous.

Option W-16.1:   Forest Lake Descent (single track, 2.5 mi./30 min., (-)1,500', moderate/difficult, moderate/technical).

Follow the marked trail to Forest Lake from the Ridge Trail down a steep, moderate/technical single track passing through thick aspens and fir trees. Branches, roots, and log drops are numerous. Exiting at the lake, a pseudo 4WD trail encircles the lake with a roller coaster ride on the lake's south side. On the northwest side of the lake, a 4WD turns right (north), drops into a drainage, then turns left following the Shaffer Fork Trail northwest down to American Fork Canyon—a slightly rutted 4WD with many imbedded rocks passing through thick aspens. After splashing through American Fork River, Dutchman's Flat is only 0.3 mile uphill.

CHUMS

"Happy cycling and keep the rubber side down"
Your friends at Chums Eyeglass Retention

Keep a smile on your face—leave no trace

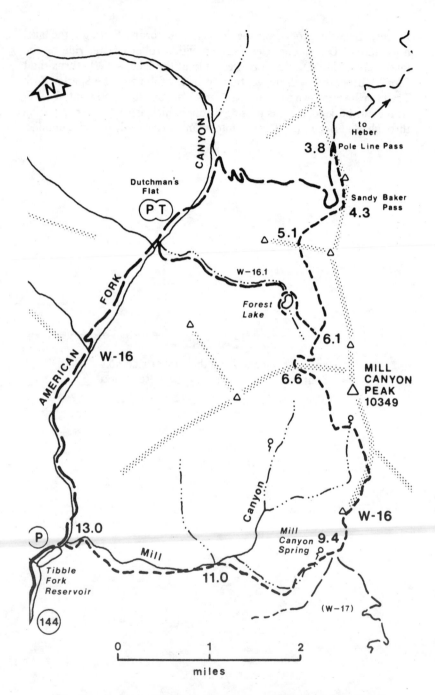

Upper American Fork Canyon—Mill Canyon Peak

Mud Springs Trail

Trail Number:	W-17 (Lower American Fork Canyon Ridgeline)
Location:	Ridgeline east of American Fork Canyon between Mill Canyon Springs and the Alpine Scenic Highway Pass.
Access:	See Mill Canyon Peak Trail. Instead of turning left to Tibble Fork Reservoir at the North Fork sign, continue east on S.R. 92 for about 6.0 miles (past Timpooneke Campground) to the summit of the Scenic Highway, just before the turnoff for Cascade Springs.
Parking:	On the south side of the pass.
Trailhead:	Directly opposite the parking area, a trail heads north signed for Ridge Trail #157, Mill Canyon Peak, and Pole Line Pass.
Type:	Loop, single track, 4WD, and paved.
Land Status:	U.S.F.S.
Maps:	U.S.G.S. 7.5' Quad.: Aspen Grove, Utah.
Length/Time:	11.2 mi./2 hr. 15 min.
Elevation Changes:	
High:	8,350' (Mill Canyon Spring)
Low:	7,000' (Cascade Springs Road)
Change:	1,350'
Trailhead:	8,060' (Note: cumulative elevation gain is +2,000'.)
Overall Difficulty:	Moderate/difficult.
Technical Difficulty:	Moderate/technical.

DIFFICULTY NOTED is with respect to the 4.2 miles of single track from the trailhead to Mill Canyon Springs. This portion is a narrow, often

Impossible to escape the prominence of Mt. Timpanogos.

deeply incised single track , and contains sections of abundant loose and imbedded rocks, a few fallen trees, and a half dozen steep climbs. 4WD and paved portions are easy/moderate downhills and uphills, respectively. Excellent views of the Alpine Ridge to the north, Box Elder Peak and Mt. Timpanogos to the west, and Provo and Lightning Peaks to the south highlight this ride.

Description

Opposite the parking area at the Alpine Scenic Highway Pass, a single track signed for Mill Canyon Peak, Tibble Fork Trail, and Pole Line Pass heads north and immediately crosses a small meadow. Important: Follow the left (west) fork skirting around the perimeter of the meadow, down a small hill, then up the first of several moderately difficult climbs to come. Do not cross the meadow on a path heading northeast. About 1.0 mile into the ride, on top of another hill, the trail splits again: to the west a path drops downhill toward the Scenic Highway, to the northeast the main trail drops down a short, steep, technical hill over several large fallen trees then into a large clearing (**m 1.1**) signed for the Pine Hollow Trail (west) and the Ridge Trail #157 (north).

Head north along the Ridge Trail, up a long, difficult, 0.5 mile climb on a narrow, incised single track containing patches of loose dirt and rocks. Expect to walk portions. Cresting the hill, you are treated to a unique view of Mt. Timpanogos. From this angle and elevation you peer deep into the glaciated bowls and valleys of Woolly Hole and Pica Cirque and up the Giant Staircase into Timpanogos Basin. Casting a shadow over this is the long, jagged Timpanogos Ridgeline, an arête formed by the joining of several glacial headwalls.

Descend another moderately difficult and technical hill northeast (downed trees crossing the path are numerous) into a clearing signed Mud Spring #173 (left) and Ridge Trail #157 (right, **m 1.8**).

Once again, follow the Ridge Trail along a deeply incised path, up another short, very steep section, and past the junction for the Tibble Lake Trail (dropping steeply to the northwest).

Onward for more of the same—up and down along the ridge until it exits onto a 4WD marking the highest point on the ride (**m 4.2**). Essentially flat (what a treat), the 4WD heads north 0.5 mile to a large clearing where several trails intersect, denoting Mill Canyon Spring (**m 4.8**). Mill Canyon Trail #040 branches west, the Ridge Trail continues up toward Mill Canyon Peak to the northeast, and a 4WD dirt/gravel road (return route) descends to the southeast. This 4WD drops 1,000' over 2.6 miles, joining with the Cascade Springs Road (paved, **m 7.4**). Loose gravel, sharp turns, and severe washboard are common. It is an easy descent but use caution just the same.

Turn right on the paved road for a soothing 0.5 mile downhill glide, then conclude the loop with a long, easy to moderately difficult grind 3.0 miles back to the Scenic Highway (turn right and uphill for a few hundred yards to return to the summit parking area).

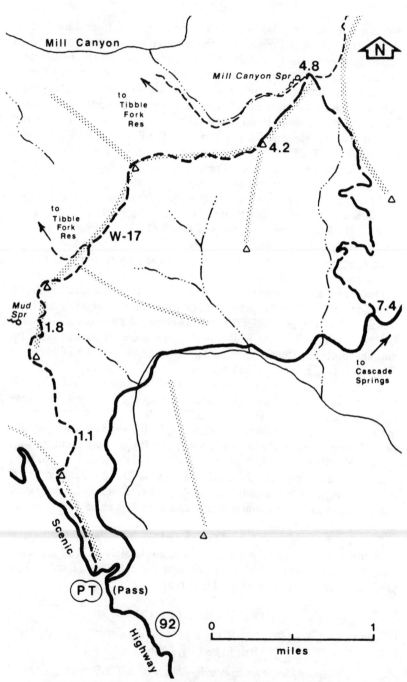

Lower American Fork Canyon—Mud Springs

Mt. Timpanogos

Trail Number:	W-18
Location:	American Fork Canyon/Mount Timpanogos.
Access:	See access for Mill Canyon Peak Trail. Travel 3.3 miles east on S.R. 92 (Alpine Scenic Highway) past the North Fork turn off, turn right for Timpooneke Campground.
Parking/Trailhead:	A parking area is provided at the head of the Timpooneke Trail for the Mt. Timpanogos Wilderness Area (remember bikes are not allowed in designated Wilderness Areas).
Type:	Out and back, 4WD.
Land Status:	U.S.F.S.
Maps:	U.S.G.S. 7.5' Quad.: Timpanogos Cave, Utah.
Length/Time:	8.6 mi./1 hr. 30 min. (one way). Allow the same amount of time for the return trip.
Elevation Changes:	
High:	8,600' (west flank of Mt. Timpanogos)
Low:	7,360' (trailhead)
Change:	1,240'
Overall Difficulty:	Moderate.
Technical Difficulty:	Minor/moderate.

OVERALL, THIS RIDE FOLLOWS a good 2WD/4WD but with just enough imbedded rocks to keep you up and out of your saddle—while trying to absorb the shock—for the majority of the ride. Excellent views of the Utah Valley and, of course, classic textbook alpine glaciation of the east side of Mt. Timpanogos highlight this ride.

Mt. Timpanogos

Description

About 0.2 mile past the parking area, the paved road turns to dirt/gravel and is passable by 2WD but is a rough ride. By far the most scenic stretch, the next 2.0 miles affords views deep into the scoured valleys and hanging glacial bowls of "The Giant Staircase," Woolly Hole, and Pika Cirque on the northeast flank of Mt. Timpanogos. But the beauty of Mt. Timpanogos also lies in its heavily forested slopes, making this a spectacular autumn ride on a road carpeted with golden aspen leaves backdropped by dark hues of evergreen.

Rounding a small ridge (m 2.1), the trail turns southwest passing beneath the precipitous head of Rock Canyon, and then wraps around to the west flank of Timpanogos rising gently to m 5.0. Although much of the ride thus far has been fairly easy and fast cruising, slow down to catch a glimpse of Box Elder Peak towering above American Fork Canyon to the north, with Lone Peak hiding behind its shoulder.

Mile 5.0, denoted by a corral and F.R. 321 branching west, marks the highest point of the trail. Remember the rule of thumb, "What goes down must come back up, eventually."

From here the road descends 1,000' over the next 3.6 miles, hugging the western flank of Timpanogos to a large clearing bound by a thick grove of aspens (m 8.6). Many 4WD trails branch to either side, but most give out shortly. Watch for rocks in the main trail as they are more numerous hereafter. More importantly, observe the ever changing face of Mt. Timpanogos peering down from above, although the true summit is not visible until almost the end of the trail. Even though a few bike tracks appear to have descended Grove Creek Trail #048, riding back up this ridiculously steep side trail seems impossible.

At m 8.6, F.R. 056 turns west across the clearing, whereas the main 4WD drops suddenly then continues around the mountain's southwest flank, a journey of unknown difficulty. Enough downhill, take a break beneath the canopy of aspens before returning on the same route.

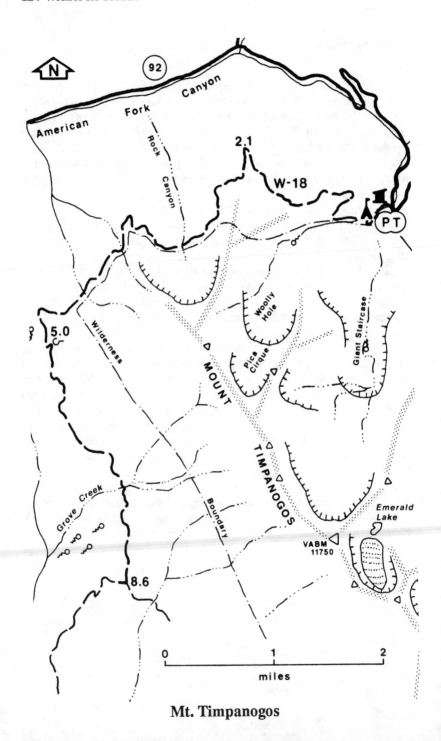

Mt. Timpanogos

Cascade Springs

Trail Number:	W-19
Location:	Cascade Springs, about 9 miles east of Timpanogos Caves National Monument or about 8 miles southwest of Heber City.
Access:	See Mill Canyon Peak and Mud Springs trails for access into American Fork Canyon. From the North Fork turn off, continue east then southeast on S.R. 92 for about six miles to the Alpine Scenic Highway Pass. Just over the pass, turn left (east) on the Cascade Springs Road then about seven miles to the Cascade Springs Parking area.
	From the Heber Valley side, head east from the traffic light in the center of Heber City on S.R. 113 S. (100 S.) about three miles into Midway. Turn left on S.R. 113 S. toward Charleston. After 1.8 miles, turn right (west) on S.R. 220 just before the railroad crossing (signed for Cascade Springs). Now, after 0.5 mile, turn right (north) then left (west) onto the dirt 2WD Cascade Springs Road (signed for Wasatch Mountain State Park and Cascade Springs). This dirt road rises about six miles then drops down to the Cascade Springs parking area.
Parking:	Provided at Cascade Springs.
Trailhead:	Directly opposite (east) of the parking area on the dirt 2WD Cascade Springs Road (signed for Heber).
Type:	Loop, 2WD and 4WD.
Land Status:	Wasatch Mountain State Park and U.S.F.S.
Maps:	U.S.G.S. 7.5' Quad.: Aspen Grove, Utah.
Length/Time:	9.5 mi./1 hr. 30 min.

Elevation Changes:

High:	7,200'	(ridgeline east of Cascade Springs)
Low:	5,880'	(junction of 4WD and 2WD near Charleston)
Change:	1,320'	
Trailhead:	6,250'	
Overall Difficulty:	Moderate.	
Technical Difficulty:	Moderate.	

ONE HALF OF THIS RIDE is on a well maintained 2WD dirt/gravel road, and one half on an eroded, moderately technical 4WD (mostly downhill).

Aside from more fantastic views along the trail of Mt. Timpanogos, Deer Creek Reservoir, and placid Heber Valley, Cascade Springs is a unique ensemble of sparkling emerald pools rimmed by broad lily pads and tall grasses, literally the birthplace of a river where crystal clear ground waters seep from the hillsides. Do take the time to stroll along the boardwalk meandering through the many pools and cascading springs.

Description

At the Cascade Springs parking area, look due east up an intimidating hill marked with signs for Heber and Midway. This ride offers no warm-up, starting with a 1,000 foot climb in just less than the first mile. Fortunately, the first 0.8 mile is on a well graded, smooth 2WD providing excellent traction; unfortunately, the steepest section, "The Wall," is the last 0.1 mile of this climb. Attack it before you get too psyched out. Surmounting "The Wall" (**m 0.8**), use the view of Mt. Timpanogos as an excuse to stop and catch your breath.

The uphill continues on a severely eroded 4WD branching left (north) where the next 0.5 mile is moderate/difficult and moderate/technical due to short, steep slopes, deep ruts, and loose rocks. After this somewhat arduous section, the trail becomes much smoother as it gently contours the ridgeline north, passes through thick scrub oak along the way, then intersects Cummings Parkway—a 2WD dirt road (**m 2.6**). This junction is also noted as **m 3.0** under the Upper Provo Deer Creek Trail (W-20). To the right (east) a 4WD drops through scrub oak and is the main route.

The next 2.3 miles downhill is fun and exciting as deep ruts force you to hop from one side of the trail to the other in search of a smooth line. Although the descent is gradual overall, watch your speed as small patches of loose rocks sporadically coat the trail and occur when you least expect

Cascade Springs marks the birthplace of a river.

them. After winding in and out of many small side drainages, the 4WD portion ends with a triple fork in the trail (**m 4.7**). All three options exit shortly onto the dirt 2WD Cascade Springs Road, the middle trail exiting at a battered 2 mile marker.

Just over half way along the ride now (**m 4.9**), turn right (southwest) for an easy cruise up the 2WD Cascade Springs Road. Mt. Timpanogos, looming in the distance, darts in and out of view, growing majestically with each passing switchback. A light dusting of snow in early spring or late summer accents Timp's composite horizontal limestone strata. Contrast this with once flat lying limestone beds outcropping along the Cascade Springs Road, now tilted to nearly 45 degrees.

As the road crests (**m 0.8,** again), Mt. Timpanogos towers above; "The Wall" lies below at your mercy. Drop over the edge and coast back to Cascade Springs concluding the loop, but watch out for loose gravel near the switchbacks at the bottom.

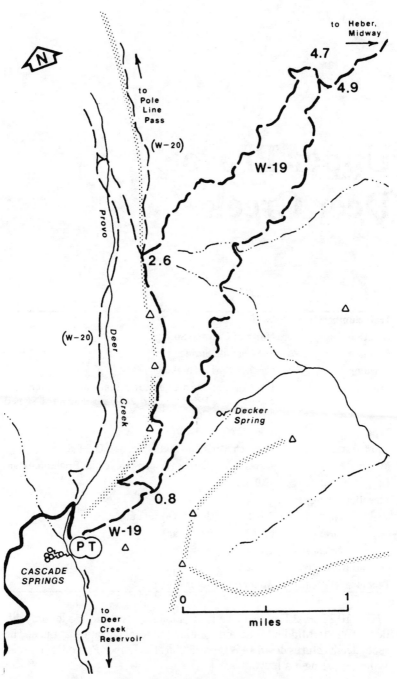

Cascade Springs

Upper Provo Deer Creek

Trail Number:	W-20
Location:	North of Cascade Springs.
Access:	See Cascade Springs.
Parking:	Cascade Springs parking area.
Trailhead:	From the parking area, return 0.3 mile on the paved Cascade Springs Road to a dirt 2WD heading north signed "Deer Creek Camp".
Type:	Loop, 2WD and 4WD.
Land Status:	Wasatch Mountain State Park and U.S.F.S.
Maps:	U.S.G.S. 7.5' Quads.: Aspen Grove and Brighton, Utah.
Length/Time:	12.0 mi./2 hr.
Elevation Changes:	

High:	8,040'	(Middle Mountain)
Low:	6,300'	(trailhead)
Change:	1,740'	

Overall Difficulty:	Moderate.
Technical Difficulty:	Minor/moderate.

THE FIRST HALF of this ride is up a long, consistent, moderately difficult 2WD to Middle Mountain, gaining the total elevation at once. The second half returns down a 4WD paralleling the Upper Provo Deer Creek Valley, crossing it a few times.

Description

The ride begins on the 2WD Cummings Parkway just north of Cascade Springs with a short, rocky, difficult climb up a distinct switchback within the first 0.3 mile. Thereafter, the 2WD climbs gently to a sharp right hand turn crossing the creek (**m 2.3**). Here, the return route enters from the north (signed Deer Creek Camp).

Rounding this switchback and now heading south, the climb becomes moderately difficult (but still technically minor—washboard), to a sharp left-hand turn on the ridgeline (**m 3.0**). Note: The two 4WD roads branching south and east are part of the Cascade Springs loop described previously.

Traveling north (still on the Cummings Parkway), the moderately difficult grind continues, with few breaks, up the ridge for two more miles. As the road contours around a small but prominent hill (**m 5.1**), it descends steeply for 0.5 mile, a well deserved break. But, as Murphy's Law would dictate, the steep downhill is followed by a steep uphill that wraps around the west flank of Middle Mountain. Where the road flattens here, an obscure 4WD branches northwest just before, then passes through a notable stand of aspens (**m 6.4**). If you find yourself passing through the aspens while continuing on the 2WD Cummings Parkway, you've missed the turnoff.

As the 4WD descends through the aspens, it switches back south following the Provo Deer Creek drainage, passes a side trail signed Pots Hollow, crosses the creek several times, then skirts around a few beaver dams as the valley widens downstream. After swimming through or preferably walking around one last, large, deep water hole, the trail splits (**m 8.8**). To the right and uphill it exits at the Little Deer Creek Campground; to the left and downhill it passes just below the campground. Both routes join together shortly then exit onto the Cummings Parkway below where it crosses the creek (noted as **m. 2.3** previously). Follow the 2WD downhill for 2.5 miles back to Cascade Springs to complete the ride.

(Note: Sheepherding is common in the Upper Provo Deer Creek drainage. If sheep are present, pass through the herd slowly and do not run them. Also, watch out for sheep dogs as they will chase and bite anything that moves—another good reason to carry a full water bottle.)

Option W-20.1:

For a longer ride, combine the Cascade Springs and Upper Provo Deer Creek Trails creating a 21-mile pseudo-figure eight loop. Begin as you would for the Cascade Springs Trail by surmounting "The Wall," then ride the ridge north until it intersects the Cummings Parkway. Continue on the Cummings Parkway north to Middle Mountain and loop back down the Upper Provo Deer Creek drainage as described above. Upon intersecting the Cummings Parkway again, just below the Little Deer Creek Campground (described as **m 2.3** above), head south back up onto the ridgeline (**m 3.0** above) then descend east and through the scrub oak down the 4WD to where it intersects the Cascade Springs dirt road. Now cruise west, up the 2WD Cascade Springs Road, then back down "The Wall" to the Springs' parking area.

Option W-20.2:   Wasatch Mountain State Park.

Past Middle Mountain, Cummings Parkway rises another 600 feet over 1.5 miles before intersecting with Snake Creek Road at Pole Line Pass. Snake Creek then drops northeast ten miles through Wasatch Mountain State Park to the Visitor's Center, but it is a rocky, bone-jarring 2WD road, not altogether a pleasant ride down or up. Another popular route through the park is up the Pine Creek Road into the Bonanza Flats area then on to Guardsman's Road. This 2WD is heavily traveled by motor vehicles and is often severely washboard. Although many 4WD roads and single tracks crisscross through the Bonanza Flats area, almost all exist on private property. Stop at the Visitor's Center for Wasatch Mountain State Park for additional maps and information.

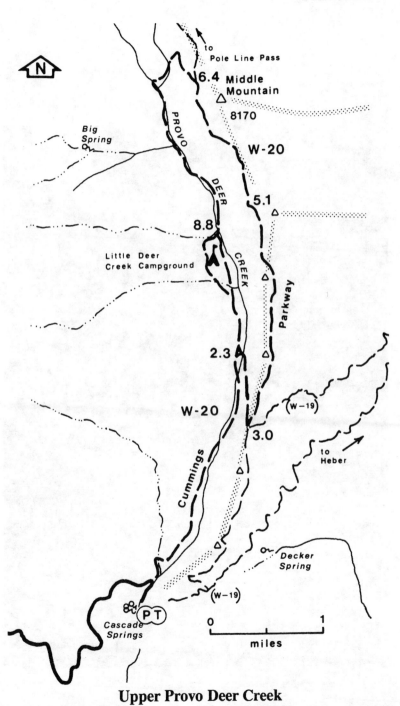

Upper Provo Deer Creek

TO MANY THE UINTA MOUNTAINS are a faraway land, an unknown world located somewhere between Salt Lake City and Denver. At only an hour drive from the Wasatch Front, the Uintas offer an untapped reservoir of recreational backcountry opportunities; they have not yet seen the onslaught of development common to the Wasatch. Pristine and secluded, this mountainous terrain still maintains numerous niches and secret hideaways far removed from the sight and sound of human influence.

For the hiker and equestrian, opportunities are endless. Trails cross broad grass covered valleys, past thousands of lakes and ponds remnant from a time when thick masses of ice blanketed the area, and up onto peaks reaching over 13,000 feet above sea level. Likewise, for the mountain biker, the Uintas' myriad crisscrossing logging roads open up a whole new world to explore. Their 2WD and 4WD roads are ideal for mountain bike travel where knobby bike tires pose little threat of erosion or environmental damage. Routes vary from a few miles to tens of miles, from an easy cruise along ridgelines and lush river banks to grueling ascents and descents. The only limit is your own endurance.

Venturing onto the many hiking trails in the delicate High Uintas requires careful consideration. Whereas the presence of mountain bikes on hiking trails among the Wasatch Mountains is generally accepted and expected, their presence in the Uintas is not as familiar. This is an area where trail etiquette should be meticulously practiced. Hiking trails in the Uintas are generally difficult bicycling routes because of steep, rocky trail conditions. Riding into the Uinta Wilderness Primitive Areas is strictly forbidden.

With numerous developed U.S.F.S. campgrounds throughout its expansive National Forest, the Uintas are an excellent choice for multi-day outings.

Access to the Western (Lower) Uintas is provided by three main routes from the Wasatch Front, two of which branch from I-80:

From the Salt Lake City metropolitan area, follow I-80 east up Parley's Canyon about 20 miles, past Park City, and turn south on U.S. 40 East for Heber City (Exit 148). Approximately 11 miles south of I-80, U.S. 189 branches left (east), connects with Francis after about seven miles (noted by its one and only blinking traffic light), then continues north through Kamas (just two miles from Francis). From the center of Kamas, S.R. 150, the Mirror Lake Scenic Highway heads east, crosses the Uinta Crest, and accesses the northern slopes of the Uinta Range (a very popular road cycling route). From the center of Francis, S.R. 35 heads east then southeast through Woodland, soon turns to a dirt 2WD thereafter, and continues to Hanna and the southern flanks of the Uinta Mountains.

To access Heber City, continue south on U.S. 40 East from the U.S. 189 junction for eight more miles. From the south end of Heber City,

U.S. 40 East angles southeast and passes Strawberry Reservoir after about 25 miles (U.S. 189 angles southwest from this junction, passes Deer Creek Reservoir, then heads down Provo Canyon back to the Southern Wasatch Front).

Realize that construction of the Jordonelle Dam, which began in the late 1980s, will eventually alter these routes when the valley is flooded. Access will be maintained to all these destinations, but the exact routing and road names were not known at the time this book went to press.

The Western Uintas and the Kamas area can also be accessed from I-80 by taking the Rockport State Park exit (# 156) about 8 miles past the Heber turn off for U.S. 40. Kamas is about 16 miles to the south.

From the Provo-Utah Valley area, access to the Uintas is via U.S. 189 through Provo Canyon. About six miles up Provo Canyon, the tram at Bridal Veil Falls rises over 1,700 feet above the canyon's bottom. Shortly thereafter, S.R. 92 (the Alpine Scenic Highway) branches north past Sundance, wraps around the eastern flanks of Mount Timpanogos, then switchbacks down into American Fork Canyon and past Timpanogos Caves National Monument. From the Scenic Highway's summit, the paved Cascade Springs Road branches east.

U.S. 189 continues up Provo Canyon past Deer Creek Reservoir and into Heber City. The Strawberry Reservoir area is accessed by traveling about 25 miles southeast on U.S. 40 East from the south end of Heber. U.S. 189/40 continues north through Heber for approximately eight miles to where U.S. 189 branches east toward the Francis/Kamas area, and U.S. 40 continues north past Park City connecting with I-80.

Upper Provo Falls along the Mirror Lake Highway.

Hoyt Peak

Trail Number:	U-1
Location:	3 miles northeast of Kamas.
Access:	From Kamas, travel north on Main Street (U.S. 189) 3.5 miles to Marion. Turn right (east) on Upper Loop Road (3200 North, next to Kamas Valley Co-Op) then travel 1.0 mile to a 2WD dirt road on the north side of Weller Storage, posted as access to Piute Creek (Hoyt Canyon).
Parking/Trailhead:	About 0.4 mile up the dirt road as it bends over a small hill, a clearing provides ample room for several vehicles. The trail is described from this point.
Type:	Loop, 4WD, and paved road.
Land Status:	U.S.F.S. and private property. Main 4WD roads are designated public access, unless otherwise posted.
Maps:	U.S.G.S. 7.5' Quads.: Kamas and Hoyt Peak, Utah
Length/Time:	15.7 mi./2 hrs. 30 min. Add 6.0 mi. and 1 hr. for Hoyt Peak option.
Elevation Changes:	
High:	8,740' (Upper Hoyt Canyon)
Low:	6,375' (Kamas)
Change:	2,365' (Note: Hoyt Peak rises to 10,230', so the overall possible elevation gain is 3,855'— the greatest elevation change of any trail presented in this book.)
Trailhead:	6,800'
Overall Difficulty:	Difficult.
Technical Difficulty:	Moderate.

HOYT CANYON IS A LONG, moderately difficult climb with only about one half mile of very difficult, very technical trail. The upper basin is generally rolling hills, while descending Wide Hollow is steep and often rocky. All are on 4WD roads. The paved road section is easy and flat. Scenic views of Park City, Deer Valley Ski Resort, and Kamas Valley, along with lush mountain vegetation mixed with broad, open alpine meadows are the attractions.

Description

Initially paralleling Hoyt Canyon Creek east, the 4WD rises gently to its first switchback (**m 1.2**), passing a sign for "Camp Aerie." The trail rises moderately to the second switchback where it then climbs steeply over very rocky conditions 0.5 mile to a third switchback and the most difficult and technical stretch. After the fourth switchback, the trail levels considerably and passes a small ridge (**m 2.4**). An optional spur extending west out onto the ridge soon turns left (south), contours the hillside 0.5 mile, then exits the National Forest (signed) before dropping sharply southwest (this may be private property).

Continuing east up Hoyt Canyon (thickly forested with oak, aspen, and conifers—a flurry of color in the fall), the road passes a spring seeping from the hillside, climbs a short rocky stretch, then crosses a locked gate/cattle guard posted, "Road closed to motorized/vehicular use for wildlife management and resource protection—USFS" (**m 2.8**). The road is now marked as F.R. 080.

Approximately 0.5 mile past the gate turn left (east) for an additional mile to the junction with the Wide Hollow Trail (**m 4.1**, the return descent). Unfortunately, this junction is unmarked, but it is distinguished by the Wide Hollow Trail (4WD) descending southeast; whereas the main road, branching left (northeast), rises gently through aspens and alpine meadows (Option U-1.1).

Descending Wide Hollow Trail is an enjoyable, exhilarating cruise for the first two miles as it passes through alpine vegetation on a smooth 4WD. Thereafter, the path descends more steeply, becomes moderate/technical due to abundant small, loose rocks, then drops into Wide Hollow itself. Squeeze through a locked, white gate posted "Kamas Wildlife Management Area," continue south down Wide Hollow through a small residential area, and exit onto the paved Mirror Lake Highway (**m 8.1**) opposite the Beaver Creek Inn (a cozy country tavern offering hot food and cold drinks).

Turn right (west) following S.R. 150 and ride 2.6 miles into the center of Kamas (if you can pass up the temptation of a double cheeseburger and a chocolate-mint shake at Dick's Drive-In, you have greater willpower than I). Head north on Main Street (U.S. 189) 3.5 miles to Marion, then another 1.5 miles back to the trailhead as described under "Access."

Option U-1.1:   Hoyt Peak (out and back, 4WD, 6.0 mi./1 hr. round trip, 1,060', moderate, moderate).

After grinding almost 2,000' up Hoyt Canyon, spend the extra hour to ramble through the high alpine basin to the base of Hoyt Peak.

From the junction with the Wide Hollow Trail (**m 4.1**, described previously), turn left (northeast) rising gently uphill along a rolling path through the aspens. As the trail curves east it splits (**m 1.4**). The left fork (main route) ascends a short, steep, rocky hill then levels—crossing a basin of sage and tall grasses dotted with patches of evergreens. At **m 1.8**, instead of continuing on the main 4WD, branch right (east) and head out into the flats, then immediately fork left (north) along an obscure 4WD which soon wraps around to the west and connects back with the main road. (Note: upon descending from Hoyt Peak stay on the main 4WD trail instead of backtracking through this 0.3 mile loop.)

Now back on the main 4WD road, turn right (north) for a 0.5 mile climb up a deeply rutted 4WD to a fence line on the ridge posted "Blasting, Keep Out, Danger" (**m 3.0**). In this small saddle, a rustic 4WD heads west ascending Hoyt Peak, perhaps a better hike than bike.

It's all downhill from here (3,400'). In general, the minor to moderately technical 4WD, descending back to the junction with the Wide Hollow Trail, is fast and exhilarating as you hop from side to side avoiding the ruts while aspens whiz by creating a flashing white strobe.

As always, allow other trail users the right of way!

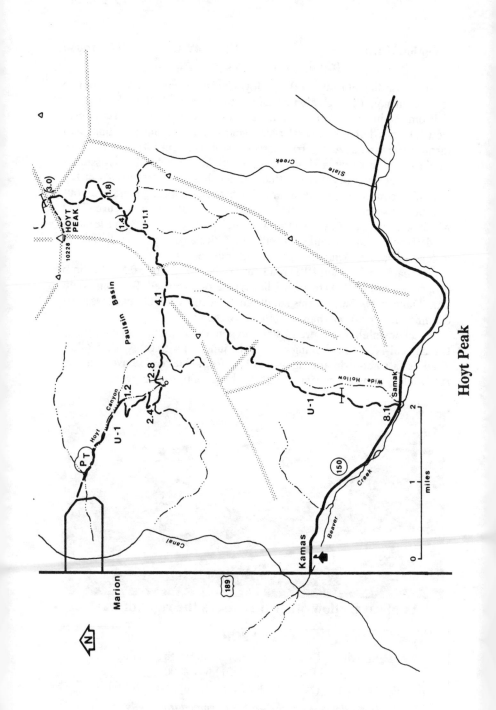

Hoyt Peak

Cedar Hollow/ Taylor Fork

Trail Number:	U-2
Location:	8 miles east of Francis (Francis is about two miles south of Kamas).
Access:	Pass east through the blinking light in Francis on S.R. 35 for 8.0 miles. Turn left (north) on Cedar Hollow Road (2WD), travel one mile up to a U.S.F.S. ATV information board for Cedar Hollow/Taylor Fork.
Parking/Trailhead:	At the ATV information board (junction of Aspen Pass and Cedar Hollow).
Type:	Loop, 4WD, and single track.
Land Status:	U.S.F.S.
Maps:	U.S.G.S. 7.5' Quads.: Woodland and Soapstone Basin, Utah.
	Cedar Hollow/Taylor Fork ATV trail map available at the Kamas Ranger Station (next to Thompson's Chuckwagon).
Length/Time:	11.4 mi./1 hr. 50 min. Add about 10 miles and 2 hours for the Cedar Loop option.
Elevation Changes:	
High:	8,700' (ridgeline)
Low:	7,200' (trailhead)
Change:	1,500'
Overall Difficulty:	Moderate/difficult.
Technical Difficulty:	Moderate/technical.

A SMALL PORTION OF THE LOOP travels on a 2WD/4WD dirt road (Cedar Hollow), whereas the majority travels on a wide single track, part

of a designated ATV trail system. Ascending and descending the ridge is moderate/difficult and moderate/technical mainly due to abundant imbedded rocks. The single track from Beaver Creek back to the trailhead is essentially flat and easy. Scenic views of the High Uintas and Pine Valley (North Fork of the Provo River) highlight this ride

Description

Unlike others, this trail begins with two options: ascending Aspen Pass, described as Option U-2.1, or ascending Cedar Hollow (easier), described here.

From the ATV information board, marking the junction of Aspen Pass and Cedar Hollow, travel northeast on the 2WD Cedar Hollow Road. As the road turns north (m 0.5), the loop's return trail enters from the right (northeast) and is blocked to motor vehicles by a large earthen berm.

Continue north up Cedar Hollow, an easy to moderately difficult climb, to the junction with Aspen Pass (m 2.7). Here the trail grades to a wide single track proceeding up Aspen Pass. After 0.5 mile, the trail splits (m 3.2): the left fork branching northwest is signed for Cedar Loop (Option U-2.2); the right fork, branching northeast and signed for Taylor Fork, is the main route. Up a short, steep section, the ATV trail passes through a fence (a gap is provided) and onto the ridgeline where the trail becomes quite rocky (m 3.8).

Descending off the ridge to the northwest, the wide path is steep and technical but a very enjoyable challenge as you weave through a few large boulders. Continuing down through tall Douglas fir, the trail flattens, passes through sapling aspens and open fields, then drops to the junction with Taylor Fork (signed, m 5.6).

Turn right and downhill where the toughest section of the ride awaits—a one mile descent on a moderately steep, extremely rocky trail. Like riding through a field of bowling balls, the pounding is severe. Correct tire pressure is crucial through here: Over inflated tires accentuate the bumpy ride and may throw you off balance, but underinflated tires raise the threat of bottoming out your rims in return for a softer ride.

Breathe a sigh of relief as the trail exits onto the Beaver Creek Trail next to another Cedar Hollow/Taylor Fork ATV information board (m 6.3).

The Beaver Creek Trail, which actually begins 2.5 miles to the west, is a popular cross country ski trail and a remarkably smooth, flat ATV/mountain bike trail. Follow the wide single track southeast as it passes behind the Shingle Creek Campground and through some rock barriers on the far side of the picnic area parking lot. About 1.7 miles from the previous ATV information board, the return trail branches to the right (south)—a faded 4WD posted with a small "Road Closed" sign (**m 8.0**). A 100 foot Ponderosa pine with a split trunk and an old fire ring also mark this turnoff. Note: The Beaver Creek Trail continues east here, descends and then crosses a rocky stream bed, and exits onto a dirt 2WD road accessing the Yellow Pine and Lower Provo River campgrounds.

The return route, an old 4WD used mainly as a cattle trail, heads south, passes through lodgepole pines, and contours below the ridgeline while staying several hundred vertical feet above Pine Valley and the meandering North Fork of the Provo River. Overall, the return trail is easy to moderately difficult, declining slightly in elevation. After crossing a fence line (**m 9.4**), the trail deteriorates in a few sections and requires some walking. Exit over the earthen berm mentioned earlier onto Cedar Hollow Road (**m 0.5**, noted earlier), then turn left and cruise a half mile back to the trailhead.

Option U-2.1:   Aspen Pass (4WD, 3.6 mi./40 min. one way, moderate/difficult, moderate)—an optional ascent for riders who don't mind pushing their bikes.

Instead of cruising up Cedar Hollow (not much of a challenge), head north up Aspen Pass on a five foot wide ATV trail. The first 1.3 miles is a consistent, moderately difficult, technically minor grind with numerous small earthen berms/speed bumps. At a tall Douglas fir tree, standing alone in a small grassy clearing, the trail turns west then immediately north and climbs 500 feet over the next 0.5 mile up a very rocky, very technical stretch, most of which is not rideable. Switching back across the drainage, the trail passes through an ATV gap in the fence line, then climbs gently for another 1.5 miles weaving in and out of the pines before connecting with the Cedar Hollow Trail at **m 2.7**, described earlier.

Option U-2.2:   Cedar Loop (combo, 4WD, 10.6 mi./1 hr. 45 min., difficult, technical).

From the junction of Aspen Pass and Cedar Hollow (**m 2.7**), head north 0.5 mile as described previously. However, follow the Cedar Loop (signed) to the northwest around a few switchbacks and up a few short, steep, rocky climbs onto the ridgeline. The smooth flat ridge trail turns south (**m 1.8**) descending on a very rocky, bone-jarring 4WD to the junction with Moon Spring (signed, **m 3.1**). Take the right fork which descends for another 0.5 mile to a trail junction signed Beaver Creek (right-north, **m 3.7**). Since this junction is obscure, if you continue straight out onto the Corral Loop past a round water tank, you missed it.

Following the Beaver Creek sign north, the trail begins a 1.7 mile, 600 foot climb back onto the ridgeline. With many short, steep, rocky ascents along the way, this section is very difficult, and turning around now is not practical. The trail now drops off the ridge to the west, soon switches north and uphill at the junction for Red Pine (signed, **m 5.9**), loops around the north side of the ridge down a steep, technical stretch, then passes a few prospect tailings. Past the prospects, the path is less technical but quite steep and potentially fast as it winds down the north face of the ridge. Near the bottom, fork left at a junction marked "Cedar Loop" which drops you to the Beaver Creek Trail (**m 8.8**). Turn right, cruising east on the flat Beaver Creek Trail for about 1.5 miles, to the Cedar Hollow/Taylor Fork ATV information board (noted as **m 6.3** in the main description). Complete the ride as described above.

(Note: The Cedar Loop option turns an 11.5 mile moderately difficult ride into a 19-mile *gonzo*/abusive cross country trek. Obtaining the Cedar Hollow/Taylor Fork ATV trail map from the Kamas Ranger District, before venturing out onto this route, is strongly advised.)

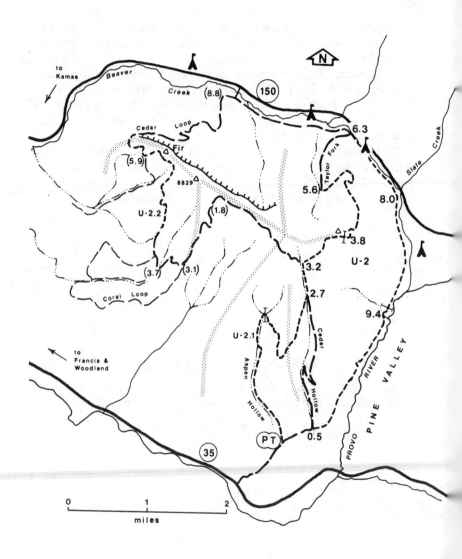

Cedar Hollow—Taylor Fork ATV Area

Soapstone Basin

Trail Number:	U-3
Location:	15 miles east of Kamas.
Access:	About 15 miles east of Kamas on S.R. 150 (Mirror Lake Highway), turn right (south) on Soapstone Road toward Soapstone Pass and Piuta MIA camp. Follow the 2WD dirt/gravel Soapstone Road (often rocky and washboard) for about two miles, then turn right (south) at the Iron Mountain Road intersection. Turn right again (southeast) and uphill at the intersection with F.R. 304 (following signs for Piuta MIA Camp and Wolf Creek), and travel 1.5 miles to Soapstone Pass.
Parking/Trailhead:	At or near Soapstone Pass.
Type:	Loop, 2WD and 4WD.
Land Status:	U.S.F.S.
Maps:	U.S.G.S. 7.5' Quads.: Soapstone Basin and Iron Mine Mountain, Utah.
Length/Time:	15.6 mi./2 hr. Add 3.0 miles and 30 min. for Option U-3.1
Elevation Changes:	
High:	9,800' (junction with Trail Hollow)
Low:	8,690' (north side of Soapstone Basin)
Change:	1,110'
Trailhead:	9,080'
Overall Difficulty:	Moderate.
Technical Difficulty:	Minor.

THIS LOOP IS AN ENJOYABLE moderate to long ride on a 2WD/4WD dirt road through a high basin setting with plenty of cruising in your higher gears. Elevation changes are minimal: rocky stretches are frequent but of little technical difficulty, making this a good beginner to intermediate ride. The optional spur to "The Bluffs" overlook offers out-standing vistas of the High Uintas and Duchesne River Valley and is strongly recommended.

Description

Soapstone Pass is the recommended starting point of this ride not only because it provides convenient parking, but because it offers numerous overnight camping sites (but no facilities) for those who wish to make the Uintas a multi-day event. At the pass, ride east on F.R. 089, a dirt and gravel 4WD rolling over low lying hills, for **4.5** miles to the junction for Cold Spring and Iron Mine Creek (signed). The main route continues left (north) along a slightly rougher 4WD. Although the road is rutted in spots, technical difficulty is only minor to moderate. As the road bends north, several 4WD roads branch to the east, closing small side loops out toward Lightning Ridge and Mill Fork.

Approximately **8.0** miles into the ride, the Trail Hollow Road (signed) forks to the right (east). Highly recommended, this 1.5 mile spur (Option U-3.1) rises to The Bluffs overlooking a staggering 2,700 foot precipice above the Duchesne River Valley.

Back on the main route, the 4WD (now F.R. 304) continues northwest then west for more of the same—low rising hills and long coasting downhills through open meadows and patches of dense fir trees. About 5.0 miles ahead, the trail parallels then crosses Soapstone Creek, and finally intersects with the Soapstone Road (F.R. 037, **m 14.0**).

The ride concludes, unfortunately, with a jarring, 1.7 mile, moderately difficult climb back to Soapstone Pass. Starting at the lower intersection of F.R. 037 and F.R. 304 (**m 14.0**) puts this hill at the beginning of the ride, but Soapstone Pass offers more secluded parking.

Option U-3.1:   Trail Hollow—The Bluffs Overlook (out and back, 4WD, 1.5 mi./15 min. one way, 300', moderate, moderate).

Turn right (east) on Trail Hollow from the main loop road (**m 8.0**). Shortly thereafter, fork left beginning a one mile uphill. Turn left again for "The Bluffs" (signed) up a short, very steep hill covered with loose gravel to the overlook. 2,700 feet below the Duchesne River meanders through its broad, green, flood plain valley. The gorge exposes gray lime-stone cliffs (Mississippian Age) comprising "The Bluffs" and orange-red

**From atop the Bluffs, the Duchesne River Valley
lies 2,700 feet below.**

sandstone walls (Precambrian Uinta Mountain group?) across the valley to the east. To the north, the High Uinta Peaks (Mounts Watson, Hayden, Bald and Aggassiz) cap the horizon, an impressive display of glacial and fluvial erosional forces.

Option U-3.2:

Although not explored extensively, several 4WD roads extend west from Soapstone Pass toward Soapstone Mountain and past the Piuta MIA Camp (private) toward Noblett's Creek.

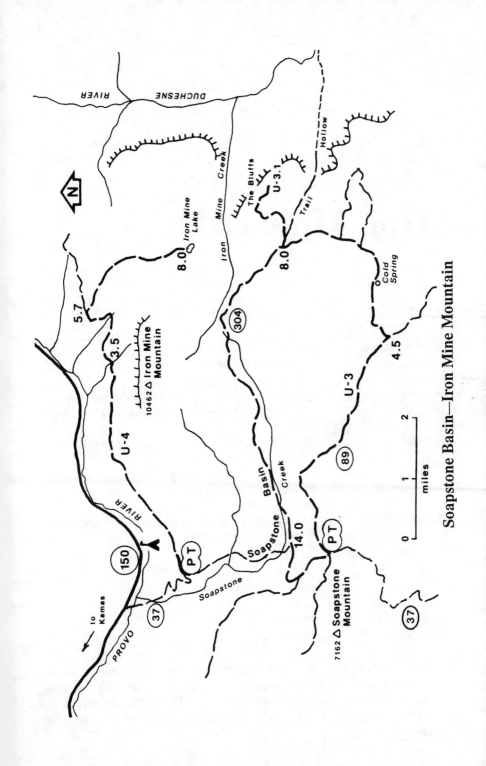

Soapstone Basin—Iron Mine Mountain

Iron Mine Lake

Trail Number:	U-4
Location:	15 miles east of Kamas.
Access:	Same as for Soapstone Basin.
Parking/Trailhead:	Park at or near the junction of Iron Mine Road and Soapstone Road, about two miles from the Mirror Lake Highway.
Type:	Out and back, 4WD.
Land Status:	U.S.F.S.
Maps:	U.S.G.S. 7.5' Quads.: Soapstone Basin and Iron Mine Mountain, Utah. See trail map for "Soapstone Basin" (U-3)
Length/Time:	8.0 mi./1 hr. 15 min. (one way). Allow the same amount of time for the return trip.
Elevation Changes:	
High:	9,850' (Iron Mine Lake Road)
Low:	8,420' (trailhead)
Change:	1,430'
Overall Difficulty:	Moderate.
Technical Difficulty:	Moderate.

THIS 4WD CONTAINS ABUNDANT imbedded rocks making for an often bone-jarring, palm-bruising ride. A short section near the lake, where the road crosses barren outcrop, is technical and may require some walking. Yet, Iron Mine Lake is secluded and peaceful and well worth the trip.

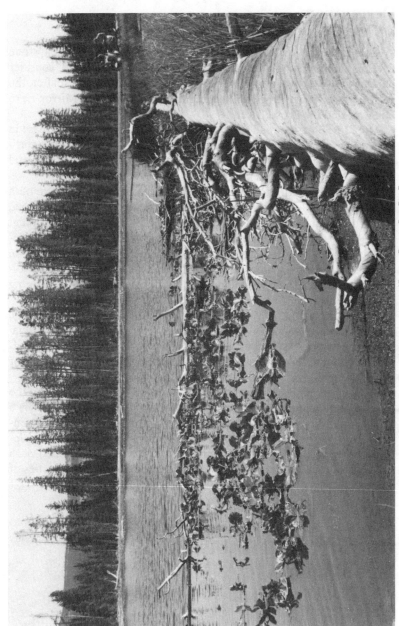

Iron Mine Lake—tranquil and secluded.

Description

Since the first mile up Iron Mine Road from its junction with Soapstone Road is moderate/difficult and full of small imbedded rocks, consider parking above this stretch where the road flattens slightly. Thereafter, the road levels to a gentle grade hugging the cliffs above the Mirror Lake Highway and the Provo River.

After **3.5** miles, the road steepens slightly with a noticeable increase in imbedded rocks. Crossing a drainage (minor flow), the road turns north climbing moderately before breaking out to a broad sage, pinon, and juniper covered plateau (**m 5.7**).

Turn right (south) for Iron Mine Lake along an initially smooth dirt/sand 4WD, an easy cruise. About one mile ahead, the smooth road turns to a technical, rocky path climbing a small hill—the highest point on the ride—then descends off this hill crossing barren outcrop with abundant large, loose rocks. This is the most technical section (emphasis on technical). Although many side trails branch to the east (i.e., Coyote Hollow), continue south on what appears to be the main road. The battering stops less than a mile further as the path drops to Iron Mine Lake (**m 8.0**).

The return ride is, obviously, just as bad with ascending that gnarly, rocky hill to start things off. The remaining return trip is a long gradual descent on a road just rocky enough to force you up and out of your saddle in a futile attempt to absorb the pounding. Whether ridden fast or slow, the hand-bruising, spine-compressing abuse is forever prevalent.

So, why subject yourself to such a torturous adventure? Well, in the classical style and setting of the Uinta Mountains, Iron Mine Lake is a placid, emerald jewel nestled among tall pines and quaking aspens. Encircled by thick grasses and rimmed with spreading lily pads, the lake captures the tranquillity of the backcountry. Pack a lunch and a ground cloth and bask in the soothing rays of warmth, leaving behind the anxieties of life in the valley.

Heber Mountain

Trail Number:	U-5
Location:	12 miles east of Heber City.
Access:	East on S.R. 35 (through the blinking light in Francis) for 9.5 miles, through Woodland, to the end of pavement. Continue on S.R. 35 (dirt 2WD) 4.8 miles to Mill Hollow (F.R. 054). Turn right (south) up Mill Hollow Road 3.8 miles to Mill Hollow Reservoir.
Parking/Trailhead:	Mill Hollow Reservoir Campground. Day use parking provided.
Type:	Combination, 2WD, and 4WD.
Land Status:	U.S.F.S.
Maps:	U.S.G.S. 7.5' Quads.: Heber Mountain and Wolf Creek Summit, Utah.
Length/Time:	17 mi./2 hr. 15 min.
Elevation Changes:	
High:	10,210' (Heber Mountain)
Low:	8,495' (Mill Hollow Guard Station)
Change:	1,715'
Trailhead:	8,845'
Overall Difficulty:	Moderate.
Technical Difficulty:	Minor/moderate.

OVERALL, THE HEBER MOUNTAIN TRAIL is an easy to moderately difficult cruising ride. Most of the elevation is gained on the graded (sometimes washboard) 2WD Mill Hollow Road. 4WD roads pass along broad, open, grass and sage covered ridges in and out of patches of trees. Sheepherding is common in this area.

Description

Mill Hollow Reservoir, sitting at 8,845 feet, marks the beginning of this ride and provides both ample day use parking and overnight camping facilities. Ride 3.0 miles up the long, moderately difficult 2WD Mill Hollow Road (F.R. 054) to its crest on Duchesne Ridge. A large wooden U.S.F.S. trail sign indicates Wolf Creek Summit and Hanna to the left (east) along the ridge, Heber and Lake Creek Summit to the right.

Proceed right (southwest), downhill slightly, along F.R. 054 for 0.2 mile, then turn right (north) up onto a low ridge following signs for Mount Heber. On the ridge (**m 3.3**), F.R. 096 branches left (signed for Mount Heber and Camp Hollow); whereas F.R. 052 branches right toward Campbell Hollow, the return trail.

**Peaks of the High Uintas backdrop vistas from
Heber Mountain and Duchesne Ridge.**

Follow F.R. 096 to the left (southwest) along the undulating ridge for about 1.5 miles and past the trailhead for the Little South Fork Trail (signed and closed to motor vehicles) to the turnoff for the Heber Mountain Trail (**m 4.7**). This junction is quite vague and unmarked on topographic maps but noted by a solitary 4x4 post that was probably a trail marker at one time.

The Heber Mountain Trail (4WD, and possibly abandoned) branches left uphill, parallels the main 4WD a short distance, then turns south ascending the gently rising ridge. Although several side trails branch to the right, stay on the main road following the ridgeline southwest (moderately difficult and minor to moderately technical). The trail ends on top of Heber Mountain (**m 7.0**), offering an unparalleled view of the eastern slopes of Mount Timpanogos, Provo Peak, and lesser peaks of the central Wasatch to the northwest. Return on the same route back to the junction with F.R. 052 for Campbell Hollow (**m 3.3**).

Now, shift into a higher gear and follow F.R. 052 northeast (again an easy cruise along a broad undulating ridge) for about 2 miles before branching right on F.R. 122 down Campbell Hollow (**m 12.8**). Campbell Hollow steepens slightly for a fairly smooth, fast coast before joining with Mill Hollow Road just above the Guard Station (**m 15.7**). Turn right and climb back up Mill Hollow Road one mile back to the reservoir.

Option U-5.1:   Buck Hollow Ridge (out and back, 4WD, 4.3 miles/50 min. one way, 500', easy/moderate, minor/moderate).

Instead of branching south for Heber Mountain, continue straight on F.R. 096, descending gradually but consistently through the pines and open meadows. After zigzagging northwest across a few broad, flat ridges, the 4WD extends north onto Buck Hollow Ridge (signed). Although the road continues further, it was not explored.

[Note: The Heber Mountain Trail, described here, can be split easily into smaller trips by using the junction of F.R. 096 and F.R. 052 (signed Mount Heber/Campbell Hollow) as a pivot (**m 3.3**).]

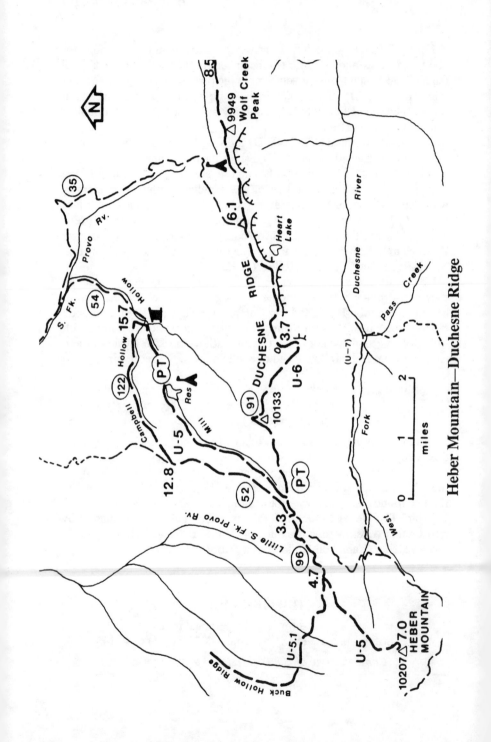

Heber Mountain—Duchesne Ridge

Duchesne Ridge

Trail Number:	U-6
Location:	12 miles east of Heber City.
Access:	Same as for the Heber Mountain Trail
Parking/Trailhead:	At or near the junction of Mill Hollow Road (F.R. 054) and Duchesne Ridge Road (F.R. 091), about 3 miles past Mill Hollow Reservoir.
Type:	Out and back, 2WD, and 4WD.
Land Status:	U.S.F.S.
Maps:	U.S.G.S. 7.5' Quads.: Heber Mountain and Wolf Creek Summit, Utah. See trail map for "Heber Mountain" (U-5).
Length/Time:	8.5 mi./1 hr. 15 min. (one way). Allow the same amount of time for the return trip.
Elevation Changes:	
High:	10,080' (Peak-10133)
Low:	9,545
Change:	535'
Trailhead:	9,740'
Overall Difficulty:	Easy/moderate.
Technical Difficulty:	Minor.

THE MAJORITY OF THIS ROUTE travels a graded 2WD rising and falling gently along the ridge. Small amounts of 4WD are moderately difficult, but still technically minor. Duchesne Ridge, broad and flat to the north, drops off as sheer 2,000 foot cliffs to the West Fork of the Duchesne River to the south.

Description

The Duchesne Ridge Road, a delightful high speed cruise, begins at the junction of Mill Hollow Road and Duchesne Ridge. Here, a large wooden sign directs you east along the ridge toward Wolf Creek Summit and Hanna on F.R. 091. The entire ride is a series of easy to moderately difficult undulating hills crossing over grass and sage covered meadows and through small patches of dense evergreen. In large part, the ridge consists of tan to pink Tertiary pyroclastic rocks (an explosive volcanic rock composed of chaotic chunks welded in a finer matrix of glass shards or pumice-like material) overlying Paleozoic sedimentary rocks.

About four miles along the ridge the road passes Yellow Lake (**m 3.7**), a small pond of a peculiar yellow-green color much like that of automobile antifreeze. Take a walk around the lake and note the great number of salamanders. Past the lake the road drops gently into a broad saddle, then rises again onto a wide plateau where the 2WD turns 90 degrees to the north (**m 6.1**).

If continuing on the 2WD north, it soon turns east, descends through some steep switchbacks to Wolf Creek Summit Campground, and connects with S.R. 35 (2WD dirt). Although this is a plausible route, follow the ridgeline east along a vague 4WD extending from this sharp northward bend in F.R. 091. Understand that this junction is not altogether obvious. Only a small campsite-like clearing on the northside of the road and a number of small "Road Closed" signs on the south side mark the intersection. Also, from this intersection Heart Lake lies beneath Duchesne Ridge to the south. Its shape changes with the season from heart shaped, during high water in the springtime, to butterfly shaped, during lower water in late summer.

The 4WD, heading east along the ridge, contours around the north side of Wolf Creek Peak, through thick stands of evergreen, then comes to a fence line marking the end of the trail (**m 8.5**). Actually, the 4WD continues past the fence line for about 1.5 miles, but fades out to a rocky game trail that is not rideable for all practical purposes.

The return route is exactly the opposite.

BICYCLE UTAH

For a free "Bicycle Utah Vacation Guide" and bike route guides to Utah's nine travel regions
1 (800) 453-1360 ■ in state (649-6100)

Greatest bicycling on earth

Roundy Basin/ Low Pass

Trail Number:	U-7
Location:	About 14 miles east of Heber City.
Access:	Same as for the Duchesne Ridge Trail. At the junction of Mill Hollow Road and Duchesne Ridge, turn right (west) downhill for 2.6 miles on F.R. 054 to the West Fork of the Duchesne River.
Parking/Trailhead:	At or near the junction of Mill Hollow Road and the West Fork of the Duchesne River Road (F.R. 054 and F.R. 050, respectively).
Type:	Loop, 2WD and 4WD.
Land Status:	U.S.F.S.
Maps:	U.S.G.S. 7.5' Quad.: Heber Mountain and Wolf Creek Summit, Utah.
Length/Time:	17.7 mi./2 hr. 30 min.
Elevation Changes:	
High:	10,050' (Roundy Basin)
Low:	8,400' (West Fork of Duchesne River at Pass Creek)
Change:	1,650'
Trailhead:	9,100'
Overall Difficulty:	Moderate.
Technical Difficulty:	Minor/moderate.

THE MAJORITY OF THIS RIDE is on 2WD/4WD roads with no to minor technical difficulty, an enjoyable high speed cruise with much of the time cranking your higher gears. However, the last 1.5 mile descent from Low Pass to the West Fork of the Duchesne River is along a steep, rocky, moderate/difficult, moderate/technical 4WD trail. Also, riding up the West Fork is moderate/difficult—a four mile grind where small imbedded rocks are numerous but water crossings are few and of no great difficulty. Unfortunately, these difficult sections are at the end of the loop, and it is not practical to ride the loop in reverse.

Description

Beginning at the junction of Mill Hollow Road and the West Fork of the Duchesne River (F.R. 054 and F.R. 050, respectively), travel southwest up F.R. 054 (an easy dirt/gravel 2WD road with minor washboard) to Lake Creek Summit (signed, **m 1.8**). Turn left (south) on F.R. 083 toward Strawberry Valley and Currant Creek (signed) along more smooth 2WD. Continue left (south) on F.R. 083 from where it joins with F.R. 049 (**m 2.3**). (Note: F.R. 049, branching west, eventually connects with Strawberry River via Bald Knoll, but stay on F.R. 083 south to continue this loop.)

F.R. 083, a luxurious meandering cruise through alpine meadows and lush basins, gently contours the base of a long ridge extending north from Currant Creek Peak then drops into Roundy Basin to the base of the peak.

On the east flank of Currant Creek Peak, turn left (east) on F.R. 080 toward Red Creek Mountain (signed, **m 5.4**). Note: F.R. 083 continues to the west eventually dropping down to Currant Creek Reservoir, but it is much too far out of the way. Descend the winding road (F.R. 080) east into the upper reaches of the Left Fork of Currant Creek, then up a gradual rise onto the ridgeline above Becky and Buck basins. A less traveled but smooth 4WD, this trail travels along a sage and grass covered ridge, again a rolling cruise offering views of the precipitous Duchesne Ridge to the north and intermittent glimpses of Currant Creek Reservoir to the south. A series of peculiar rock cairns varying from 3 feet to 10 feet tall cap the barren ridge, and, interestingly, all fall in a straight line. There are no plaques nor markers to explain their purpose.

Pass a small corral on the right (**m 7.9**), wrap around the top of Scotty Basin and Coyote Ridge extending to the south, and descend the winding trail to Low Pass (**m 11.0**), marked by a cattle guard and a fence line (F.R. 080 continues straight, up and along the ridge).

Turn left (north and downhill) on a 4WD passing through a broad clearing. The road immediately turns east, passes another corral, and then past a couple of rustic cabins. After this, the road turns left (north), becomes rougher (moderately technical) and less distinct, and descends 0.5 mile before turning sharply to the right (east).

Although this 4WD continues east here and back into aspens, turn left (north and downhill) about 100 feet past this sharp right hand turn on an abandoned 4WD that drops down a very short but *very* steep hill through the dense trees and soon exits at a small flowing creek. A triple beaver dam lies just upstream (**m 13.2**). All of these subtle turns can be confusing and occur over a short distance, thus a 7.5' topographic map is valuable to identify changes in terrain, even though the trails are not labelled correctly through here.

Follow this very rough 4WD trail (moderate/technical) down Pass Creek, crossing the creek several times, across the west fork of the Duchesne (very deep and rocky, prepare to get wet if you attempt to ride through), and up onto the Duchesne River Road (F.R. 050, **m 13.8**) at the Pass Creek Trail Sign.

Complete the loop with a 4.0 mile, moderate/difficult, bumpy ride up the West Fork to the junction with F.R. 054. Take your time, have patience, and enjoy the scenery. The last four miles back to the trail's beginning is a long consistent grind.

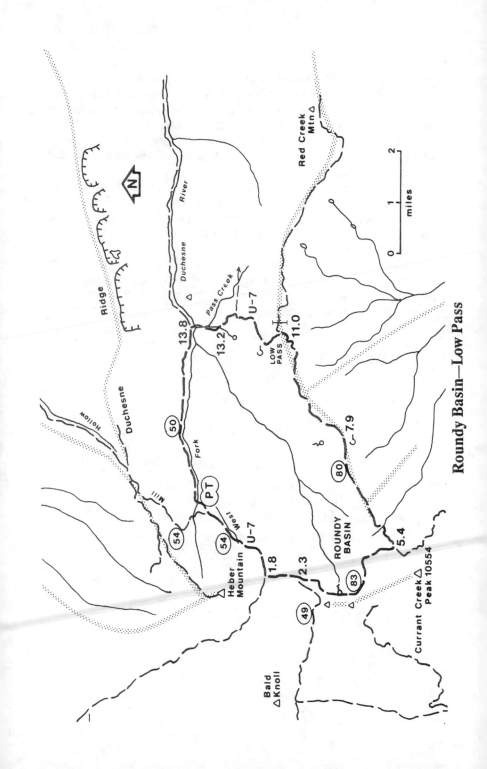

Roundy Basin—Low Pass

Strawberry River/ Mill B Canyon

Trail Number:	U-8
Location:	19 miles southeast of Heber City, north of Strawberry Reservoir.
Access:	Travel about 19.0 miles southeast of Heber City on U.S. 40 East. Turn left on F.R. 049 (2WD, signed for Strawberry River).
Parking/Trailhead:	About one mile north on F.R. 049 from U.S. 40, park at the junction with Willow Creek (F.R. 092).
Type:	Out and back, 2WD and 4WD.
Land Status:	U.S.F.S.
Maps:	U.S.G.S. 7.5' Quads.: Co-Op Creek and Heber Mountain, Utah.
Length/Time:	9.2 mi./1 hr. 30 min. (one way). Note: Allow only 1 hr. for the return trip.
Elevation Changes:	
High:	9,700' (end of trail in Upper Mill B Canyon)
Low:	7,810' (trailhead)
Change:	1,890'
Overall Difficulty:	Easy/moderate.
Technical Difficulty:	Minor.

THE FIRST HALF OF THIS RIDE is along a graded 2WD, a simple ride with only minor washboard and few rocks; the second portion is up a moderately difficult but technically minor 4WD. Both sections pass through thick forests and broad meadows, along flowing streams, and past a few beaver ponds and prime deer and elk habitat. Mill B was the sight of an old saw mill in the early 1900s.

Description

F.R. 049 paralleling Strawberry River north is a fairly smooth, flat, graded 2WD stretching 4.8 miles up to Mill B Flat. Washboard is common but rocks are few. Mill B Flat is denoted by a large wooden corral where F.R. 049 continues north crossing the river and is discussed as Option U-8.2.

At the corral, follow F.R. 093 (4WD) branching to the right (northeast) across a cattle guard then gently climbing the hillside. Thereafter, moderately difficult hills are offset by flat to gently rising sections with none being more than minor/moderate in technical difficulty. Continuing uphill past a small basin containing a few beaver ponds, the road comes to a "T" intersection (**m 8.3**). The road descending to the left is discussed as Option U-8.1. Turn right (east) for another mile uphill to a small pond sitting in a broad basin beneath the western flanks of Currant Creek Peak, marking the end of the trail (**m 9.2**).

Although the road appears to continue east toward Currant Creek Peak, it has been bulldozed and is closed to motor vehicles and unrideable. Take a little siesta in the meadow by the pond before returning on the same route.

Option U-8.1:   (Read this before doing it! Connecting trail, 4WD, single track, bushwhacking, 2.4 mi./30 min., difficult, technical, confusing).

Where the 4WD Mill B Canyon Road comes to a "T" intersection (**m 8.3**), about a mile above the beaver ponds, follow a smooth 4WD road west descending quickly to a small pond tucked away among fir and aspens. This road continues, becomes rocky, and ends at a bulldozed earthen berm by a second pond (dry, about 1 mile); turning around means a steep climb. Cross the berm and bushwhack over many fallen trees and through the thick brush for several hundred yards onto what used to be a 4WD but has since been abandoned. Soon, the trail switchbacks north; however, turn left (south) at this switchback along another faded, rough, technical 4WD (abandoned and bulldozed, again). As this path winds in and out of a small side drainage, numerous small but steep berms make this adventure technical but enticing. The path finally crosses one last large berm and exits at a road closed sign. Turn right and downhill a very short distance out onto the main Mill B Canyon Road, then turn right again to descend to Mill B Flat at the corral (**m 4.8** described earlier). Fortunately, this optional ride is downhill all the way.

Option U-8.2:   Strawberry River to Bald Knoll (out and back, 4WD, 3.8 mi./50 min. one way, 1,260', moderate/difficult, moderate).

F.R. 049 crosses Strawberry River at Mill B Flat (**m 4.8**) and continues uphill paralleling its western bank. For 2.5 miles the climb is gradual but consistent, and technical difficulty is minor. Yet, over the last mile, the road climbs moderately then steeply where imbedded rocks become more abundant near the top (marked by a "T" intersection, **m 3.8**). F.R. 049, to the right (east), continues climbing and eventually joins with the Roundy Basin/Low Pass Trail. F.R. 009, to the left (west), descends 15 miles down Center Creek and into Heber City (have a car shuttle set up if you choose this route).

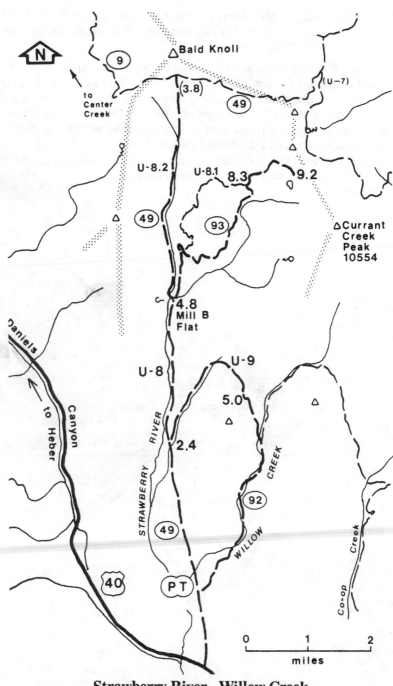

Strawberry River—Willow Creek

Willow Creek

Trail Number:	U-9
Location/Access:	Same as for Strawberry River/Mill B Canyon.
Parking/Trailhead:	Same as for Strawberry River/Mill B Canyon.
Type:	Loop, 2WD and 4WD.
Land Status:	U.S.F.S.
Maps:	U.S.G.S. 7.5' Quad.: Co-Op Creek, Utah. See trail map for "Strawberry River/Mill B Canyon" (U-8).
Length/Time:	9.0 mi./1 hr.
Elevation Changes:	
High	8,440' (top of Bjorkman Hollow)
Low:	7,810' (parking/trailhead)
Change	630'
Overall Difficulty:	Easy.
Technical Difficulty:	Minor.

EVERY NOW AND THEN, you stumble across a ride that raises an eyebrow and tickles your fancy. Willow Creek is such a ride. For the novice rider, this short loop may be a complete ride in itself. But for the advanced rider, Willow Creek is a short alternate side track upon descending from Mill B Canyon. Why? Because over the last two miles there exists seven very rideable, outrageous water crossings. Prepare to get wet.

Description

Begin this ride as you would the Strawberry River/Mill B Canyon Trail heading north up Strawberry River on F.R. 049. However, after **2.4** miles, fork right (northeast) up Bjorkman Hollow where the road rises gently with no technical difficulty for 1.5 miles. Wrapping around the northside

The faster you ride, the wetter you get.

What, no helmet?

of a small mountain, the road climbs steadily south to its highest point (m 5.0)—at most a moderately difficult ascent.

Here is where the fun begins! Gravity pulls you downhill, accelerating progressively, as you bound over a few drainage troughs. Passing Willow Creek entering from the left, you attack the first water crossing—about 6 to 12 inches deep and 20 feet wide. Stop, turn around, and splash through it again. Now, you know that water and mud wreak havoc on bearings and drive train, but this is irresistible. Keep going, there's more fun to be had—six more to be exact. Watch out for number five, the deepest and widest of them all. The loop ends with a one mile flat-out sprint back to the trailhead.

Co-Op Creek

Trail Number:	U-10
Location:	About 24 miles southeast of Heber City, north of Strawberry Reservoir.
Access:	About 24 miles southeast of Heber City on U.S. 40 East, turn left (north) on a 2WD signed for Co-Op Creek (F.R. 082).
Parking/Trailhead:	Near a large wooden corral where Chicken Creek (F.R. 245) enters from the right (northeast), immediately after turning off U.S. 40.
Type:	Loop, 4WD.
Land Status:	U.S.F.S.
Maps:	U.S.G.S. 7.5' Quad.: Co-Op Creek, Utah (also Jimmies Point, Utah for Option U-10.1).
Length/Time:	18.2 miles/2 hr. 45 min.
Elevation Changes:	
High:	9,940' (Red Ledge)
Low:	7,660' (parking/trailhead)
Change:	2,280'
Overall Difficulty:	Moderate/difficult.
Technical Difficulty:	Moderate.

ON THE WHOLE, the 4WD roads are only moderately difficult and minor to moderately technical. However, a series of steep, rocky switchbacks climb 1,000 feet in just over two miles ascending Red Ledge and Peak-Race Track, the most arduous section. An unusual conglomerate outcrops on Red Ledge—an appropriate name. Descending 6.0 miles from Red Ledge is fast and furious along a good 4WD.

Description

F.R. 082 is a well graded essentially flat 2WD road for about the first three miles heading north into the aspens. After a short rocky section, continue up Co-Op Creek (F.R. 082) past Sleepy Hollow (F.R. 149) entering from the right (**m 3.4**).

Paralleling Co-Op Creek north, the road rises gently through thick forest for two miles, rounds a tight left-hand switchback, then climbs moderately to steeply for one half mile past a Uinta National Forest sign (**m 5.8**). Technical difficulty is never more than minor/moderate. For two more miles the road weaves in and out of small side drainages and is easy to moderate in difficulty. At the junction with Sleepy Hollow/Chicken Creek (**m 7.9**) turn right (southeast) up F.R. 149. Note: F.R. 082 continues north (see Option U-10.1).

Ahead, a difficult and moderate/technical series of rock strewn switchbacks awaits, climbing about 1,000 feet in two miles. Cresting the ridge, the road contours the hillside to the base of Red Ledge and Peak-Race Track. Appropriately named, the red cliffs are composed of an unusual conglomerate (a rock consisting of pebble to boulder sized clasts cemented together in a finer sandy matrix) tainted red most likely from the finely disseminated iron mineral, hematite. These cliffs are probably part of the Tertiary Uinta Formation characterized by lake and river sedimentary deposits. The huge boulders cemented in this conglomerate are easily visible from a great distance.

Descending southwest away from Red Ledge, fork left continuing downhill on F.R. 245 toward Chicken Creek (**m 12.3**). (Note: If riding after a rain, be aware that the first one mile descent from Red Ledge is through some of the thickest viscous mud ever encountered. You may have to portage to by pass some bogs.)

For six miles Chicken Creek drops almost 2,000 feet, wrapping in and out of side drainages with short, moderately steep downhills offset by long, gentle, flat stretches. Overall, the technical difficulty along the descent is only minor to moderate, creating a fast and furious downhill ride.

After passing through a fence line, the road breaks out from the hillside for a level cruise back to the trailhead to complete the loop, a great opportunity to gear up and cool down.

Option U-10.1:   Strawberry Reservoir to Currant Creek Reservoir—the longest ride (loop, 4WD, 30 mi./4 hr. minimum, 2100', difficult, moderate/technical—*gonzo*).

The length of this ride alone justifies a difficult rating, but a near 2,000 foot climb up Race Track Creek thirteen miles into the ride validates this

Conglomerate rocks comprising the Red Ledge.

(not to mention that this ascent is very rocky and technical and requires a great deal of pushing). As described previously, ride about eight miles up Co-Op Creek (F.R. 082) to the turnoff for Chicken Creek/Sleepy Hollow (m 7.9, described previously). Continue north on F.R. 082 toward Currant Creek. Shortly, turn right (northeast) on F.R. 243 toward Currant Creek, again. (Note: F.R. 092 heads northwest toward Willow Creek here.)

After contouring the hillside for 2 miles, turn right one final time for Currant Creek on the resumed F.R. 082 to descend about 4 easy miles to Currant Creek Reservoir. For reference, a designated ATV trail to Smith Basin branches to the left. (Note: This is a point of commitment. Four miles downhill to the east is Currant Creek Reservoir, the lowest and furthest point from the trailhead. Options are: turn back, continue as described, or exit from Currant Creek Reservoir to US 40 about 18 miles southeast of Co-Op Creek.)

Upon reaching Currant Creek Reservoir, ride around the west road to Racetrack Creek (F.R. 084) marked by a brown iron gate. Now the fun begins. Ride (or push) 3.2 miles straight up Race Track Creek—no switchbacks, no breaks, lots of rocks, and steep climbs, the true meaning of "a grunt." Below the cliffs near the summit, switchback to the left on a 4WD following a sign for Trout Creek.

(Note: The roads over the next few miles do not correspond accurately with those on 7.5' topographic quadrangles.)

Traverse around the cliffs heading south and connect with F.R. 246 (signed for Layout Canyon-Water Hollow Ridge and Big Dry Hollow-Race Track Creek). Turn right (west) on F.R. 246 descending through a few tight switchbacks into Water Hollow, rise gradually onto Trout Creek Ridge, then drop to the west into Trout Creek itself (F.R. 084). Trout Creek is the final descent, the denouement, the falling climax—a moderately steep, washboard, palm-bruising, spine-compressing, paint-shaker downhill whether ridden fast or slow. After four miles of abuse, exit onto US 40. Turn right (west) for about two miles of smooth riding back to Co-Op Creek and the trailhead.

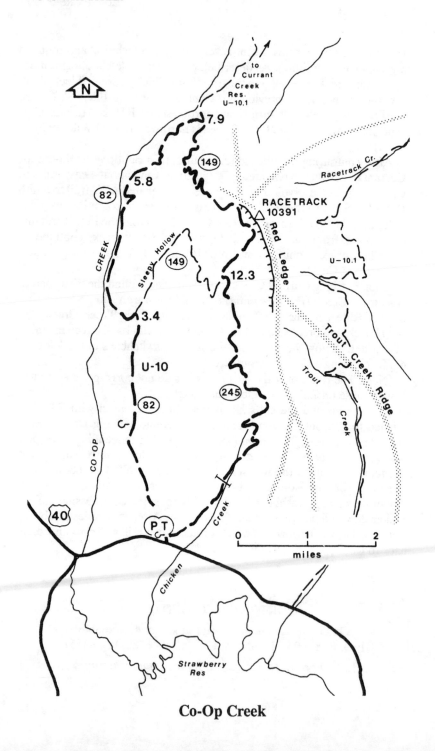

Co-Op Creek

The perfect ending to a perfect day.

Rides According to Difficulty

THE FOLLOWING IS A TABULATION of all rides according to difficulty. Remember that degree of difficulty is relative to the rides in this guide and somewhat gradational. A few rides may actually fall somewhere between categories or may fall into the next harder or easier category depending on your level of riding ability.

Easy Rides

Farmington Flats (W-2.1)
City Creek Canyon (W-5)
The "U" Trail (W-7)
Big Water to Dog Lake (W-9)
Silver Lake (W-12.1)
Silver Fork Canyon (W-12.2)
Albion Basin (W-13.1)
Upper Corner Canyon Road (W-15)
Duchesne Ridge (U-6)
Strawberry River (U-8)
Willow Creek (U-9)

Moderate Rides

Skyline Drive (W-2)
Mueller Park (W-3)
The Antennas (W-4)
Brighton to Solitude (W-12)
Mt. Timpanogos (W-18)
Cascade Springs (W-19)
Upper Provo Deer Creek (W-20)
Soapstone Basin (U-3)
Iron Mine Lake (U-4)
Heber Mountain (U-5)
Roundy Basin/Low Pass(U-7)

Difficult Rides

Skyline Trail to Ben Lomond Peak (W-1)
Meridian Peak (W-4.1)
Avenues' Twin Peaks (W-6)
Killyon Canyon (W-8)
Lake Desolation (W-9.2)
Upper Mill Creek Canyon (W-10)
Wasatch Crest Trail (W-11)
Germania Pass (W-13)
Peruvian Gulch (W-14)
Mud Springs (W-17)
Hoyt Peak (U-1)
Cedar Hollow (U-2)
Bald Knoll (U-8.2)
Co-Op Creek (U-10)

Gonzo Rides

Lewis Peak (W-1.2)
The Tram (W-14.1)
Mill Canyon Peak (W-16)
Cedar Loop (U-2.2)
Strawberry to Currant Creek Reservoir (U-10.1)

Appendix 2

United States Forest Service Offices

Wasatch-Cache National Forest
Federal Building
125 South State St.
Salt Lake City, Utah 84111
(801) 524-5030

Salt Lake Ranger District
6944 South 3000 East
Salt Lake City, Utah 84121
(801) 524-5042

Ogden Ranger District
507 25th Street
P.O. Box 1433
Ogden, Utah 84401
(801) 625-5112

Kamas Ranger District
50 East Center Street
P.O. Box 68
Kamas, Utah 84036
(801) 783-4338

Uinta National Forest
88 West 100 North
P.O. Box 1428
Provo, Utah 84601
(801) 377-5780

Pleasant Grove Ranger District
390 North 100 East
P.O. Box 228
Pleasant Grove, Utah 84602
(801) 785-3563

Heber Ranger District
125 East 100 North
P.O. Box 228
Heber City, Utah 84032
(801) 654-0470

**United States Geological Survey
Public Inquiries and Map Office**
125 S. State St.
(Federal Building-8th Floor)
Salt Lake City, UT 84111
(801) 524-5652

References

General Mountain Bike Books

Kelly, Charles, and Nick Crane. *Richard's Mountain Bike Book*. London: Richard's Bicycle Books, Ltd., 1988.

A romantic account of the origins of the modern day mountain bike from a man who lived the dreams of cycling enthusiasts in Marin County, California—from the first revamped Schwinn Excelsior "Ballooner" to its high tech hybrid of today. Also, an amusing account of biking some of the most obscure locations around the world.

Sloane, Eugene. *Eugene Sloane's Complete Book of All-Terrain Bicycles*. New York, New York: Simon & Schuster, 1985.

A comprehensive guide to the mountain bike including tips on choosing a mountain bike, riding techniques, where to bike and how to prepare for a trip, and how to repair and take care of your ATB.

Van der Plas, Rob. *The Mountain Bike Book*. San Francisco: Bicycle Books, 1984.

A detailed repair book designed specifically for mountain bikes. Includes detailed drawings and diagrams to overhaul completely every part and component on your bike.

References on Geology

Davis, Fitzhugh D. *Geologic Map of the Central Wasatch Front.* Salt Lake City: Utah Geological and Mineral Survey, 1983.

Hansen, Wallace R. *The Geological Story of the Uinta Mountains.* U.S.G.S. Bulletin 1291, 1983.

Geological history of the Uinta Mountains written for the layman. A historical account of the western explorations of John Wesley Powell and others.

Hintze, Lehi F. *Geologic Map of Utah.* Salt Lake City: Utah Geological and Mineral Survey, 1980.

Stokes, William Lee. *Geology of Utah.* Utah Museum of Natural History Occasional Paper No. 6. Salt Lake City: Utah Geological and Mineral Survey, 1986.

A fascinating chronicle of the spectacular geology that comprises the diverse and dynamic Utah scenery. Much attention is paid to the local geology of the Wasatch and Uinta mountains, a bonus for those of the surrounding Salt Lake metropolitan area. Simplistic terminology and clear writing style create a book easy and enjoyable to read for those with minimal or no geological background.

Other Biking and Hiking Guidebooks

Anderson, James. *Mountain Biker's Guide to Crested Butte.* N.p.: B & B Printers, 1988.

Detailed trail descriptions of twenty mountain bike rides, including the famous Pearl Pass to Aspen tour. Plus, background on history and folklore of one of the birthplaces of modern-day mountain biking (map separate).

Barnes, F.A., and Tom Kuehne. *Canyon Country Mountain Biking.* Moab, Utah: Canyon Country Publications, 1988.

An extensive guide to twenty-one mountain bike rides throughout the Canyonlands region, from slickrock to high mountaintop rides, plus suggestions for dozens of optional trips. Just one in a series of guidebooks to the Canyon Country of the Four Corners States.

Benefiel, Keith, and Diane Benefiel. *Mountain Bike Guide to Jackson Hole.* 17" x 22" fold out map. Wilson, Wyoming: n.p., 1987.

Brief descriptions of twenty-eight on- and off-road rides in and around Jackson Hole, Wyoming.

Campbell, Todd. *Beyond Slickrock: Rides to Nowhere.* Moab, Utah: Rim Tours Publications, 1987.

The first Canyonlands mountain bike guide highlighting 12 off-road rides in and around Moab, Utah.

Coello, Dennis. *Bicycle Touring Utah.* Flagstaff, Ariz.: Northland Press, 1988.

Another in a sequence of books dedicated to long distance touring throughout the Intermountain West. Titillating, lighthearted sketches of the people, places, and sights that separate Utah from other riding destinations—from a man who has logged over a hundred thousand bicycle miles.

Compton, Richard, and Barbara Belmont. *Highwheeling: A Mountain Biker's Guide to Aspen and Snowmass.* N.p., n.d.

Concise descriptions of off-road trips in and around Aspen, Colorado.

Kelsey, Michael. *Utah Mountaineering Guide and the Best Canyon Hikes.* Springville, Utah: Kelsey Publishing Co., 1986.

An all-star assemblage of hiking routes among Utah's mountains plus the best canyon and narrows hikes in the state.

United States Forest Service-San Juan National Forest. *Bicycle Routes to the San Juan National Forest.* N.p., n.d.

Highlights of twenty skinny and fat tire tours through the majestic San Juan Mountains near Durango, Colorado.

Veranth, John. *Hiking the Wasatch.* Salt Lake City: Wasatch Mountain Club, 1988.

A hiking and natural history guide to the Central Wasatch Mountains.

WASATCH TOURING, specialists in all forms of mountain travel, advocates the practice of "Leave No Trace." Whether on foot, ski, or bike, abiding by the guidelines of low-impact travel is instrumental in preserving the natural beauty of our public lands and maintaining continued access to the backcountry.

I am greatly indebted to Wasatch Touring and the following businesses who have sponsored this project and have recognized the importance of promoting mountain biking as an environmentally acceptable mode of backcountry travel. Only through their generosity has this book been possible. In addition to being recognized throughout this text, I sincerely extend a personal thank you to each, individually:

Alpine Sports

Bicycle Utah

The Bike Shop

Bingham Cyclery

Borge B. Andersen and Associates

Brighton Village Store & Cafe

Chums

Cole Sport

Contender Bicycles

Cycle Mania

The Eating Establishment

Gastronomy, Inc.

Golsan Cycles

Gorilla Bicycle Co.

Guthrie Bicycle

Mountain High Properties

The Pie Pizzeria

Rainbow Cycles

Reflex Sport Products

Rock & Road Cycles

The Salt Lake Roasting Co.

Sport Touring Ventures

Stout Cycles

Wasatch Touring

White Pine Touring

Wheels, Etc.

Wild Rose

Wren's Wheels and Cyclery

Utah Trails Bicycle Expeditions

Utah Valley Bicycle